GRACE ANDREWS

From Worry To *Worship*

God's Path to Living Free from Anxiety, Worry, and Stress

AN ANXIETY BOOK CHRISTIAN HEARTS WILL BE TRANSFORMED BY

© Copyright 2025 by Grace Andrews

All Rights Reserved

From Worry to Worship

God's Path to Living Free from Fear, Worry, and Anxiety

An Anxiety Book Christian Hearts Will Be Transformed By

The content contained within this book may not be reproduced, duplicated or transmitted without direct written permission from the author or the publisher.

Under no circumstances will any blame or legal responsibility be held against the publisher, or author, for any damages, reparation, or monetary loss due to the information contained within this book, either directly or indirectly.

Scripture quotations taken from The Holy Bible, New International Version® NIV®

Copyright © 1973, 1978, 1984, 2011 by Biblica, Inc.

Used with permission. All rights reserved worldwide.

Legal Notice:

This book is copyright protected. It is only for personal use. You cannot amend, distribute, sell, use, quote or paraphrase any part, or the content within this book, without the consent of the author or publisher.

Disclaimer Notice:

Please note the information contained within this document is for educational and entertainment purposes only. All effort has been executed to present accurate, up to date, reliable, complete information. No warranties of any kind are declared or implied. Readers acknowledge that the author is not engaged in the rendering of legal, financial, medical or professional advice. The content within this book has been derived from various sources. Please consult a licensed professional before attempting any techniques outlined in this book.

By reading this document, the reader agrees that under no circumstances is the author responsible for any losses, direct or indirect, that are incurred as a result of the use of the information contained within this document, including, but not limited to, errors, omissions, or inaccuracies.

ISBN 978-1-7638974-0-3 (Ebook)

ISBN 978-1-7638974-1-0 (Paperback)

ISBN 978-1-7638974-2-7 (Hardback)

Lord, as I open this book, open my heart.

Quiet the chaos.

Let Your truth sink deep into the places

where fear has made a home.

I'm listening.

I'm willing.

I'm Yours.

TABLE OF CONTENTS

Introduction	1
Exploring the Role of Scripture in Understanding Anxiety	5
Chapter 1: Understanding Anxiety Through Faith	9
Defining Anxiety in a Spiritual/Biblical Context	9
Exploring the Role of Scripture in Understanding Anxiety	11
Chapter 2: Trusting God in Stressful Times	13
Building Trust through Prayer	13
Steps to Relinquish Control to God	15
Integrating Daily Acts of Trust	16
Group Prayer to Help with Anxiety	18
Wrapping Up	19
Chapter 3: Integrating Prayer with Mental Health Tools	21
Combining Prayer with Cognitive Behavioral Techniques	21
Understanding and Confronting Spiritual Warfare	24
Designing a Prayer Routine for Mental Well-Being	26
Reflections and Takeaways	26
Chapter 4: Mindfulness and Christian Practices	29
Mindfulness Exercises with a Christian Focus	29
Creating a Holy Space for Meditation	31
Integration of Mindful Breathing with Christian Practice	34
Faith-Focused Reflection through Mindfulness	36
The "Faith Jar" for Moments of Anxiety	37
Living the Lesson	39
Chapter 5: Overcoming Anxiety with Actionable Steps	41
Developing a Daily Anxiety Management Plan	41
How to Release Trapped Emotions and Rewire Your Belief System	43

TABLE OF CONTENTS

Using Therapeutic Breathwork for Immediate Relief ... 43
Using EFT to Clear Emotions ... 47
Using EMDR to Process Trauma ... 48
Visualization to Clear Low Level Anxiety ... 49
Healing Past Traumas with God's Help ... 49
Identifying Spiritual Strongholds in Prayer ... 53
Concluding Thoughts ... 54

Chapter 6: Sustaining Long-Term Peace ... **57**
Building Habits for Lasting Change ... 57
Learning to Have a Peaceful Mindset ... 62
Incorporating Self-Care Practices ... 64
Handling Relapses of Anxiety with Grace ... 65
A Final Word on Peace ... 71

Chapter 7: Connecting with the Christian Community ... **73**
Finding Supportive Groups within Your Church ... 73
Participating in Church Events ... 74
Retreats and Conferences ... 75
Involvement in Community Service ... 76
Engagement in Workshops and Bible Studies ... 76

Chapter 8: Dietary Adjustments and Mental Health ... **79**
Understanding the Mental Health Benefits of Nutritional Changes ... 82
The Role of Nutritional Deficiencies in Mental Health ... 83
Anti-Inflammatory Foods and Their Mental Health Benefits ... 85
Understanding the Gut-Brain Connection ... 86
Steps to Integrate Dietary Changes ... 87
Insights and Implications ... 89

TABLE OF CONTENTS

Chapter 9: Balancing Faith and Emotional Struggles — 91
Identifying Conflicts Between Emotions and Religious Teachings — 91
Crafting Your Personal Action Plan — 94
Utilizing Community Support — 95
Creating Rituals for Connecting to God — 97
Flexibility in Your Christian Practices — 99
Wisdom for Moving Ahead — 101

Chapter 10: Empathy and Emotional Connection — 103
Using Empathy to Build Stronger Relationships — 103
Sharing Personal Stories to Build Connection — 105
Understanding Emotional Connection — 107
Expressing Empathy Through Actions — 109
Summary and Reflections — 110

Chapter 11: Faith's Role in Emotional Turmoil — 113
Guidelines for Using Spiritual Support in Difficult Times — 113
Creating Hope Through Faith — 116
Finding Solace in Prayer and Scripture — 117
Understanding the Transformative Power of Faith — 119

Chapter 12: Exploring Psychological and Spiritual Tools — 125
Incorporating Therapy Alongside Christianity — 125
Identifying the Right Therapist — 127
Moving Forward — 130

Chapter 13: Holistic Lifestyle Improvements — 131
Incorporating Exercise into Your Mental Health Routine — 131
Creating an Exercise Plan — 132

TABLE OF CONTENTS

Mindful Movement	133
Community Engagement	136
Developing Healthy Sleep Habits	138
Spending Time with Friends	141
Reflections	144
Chapter 14: Vulnerability	**145**
Vulnerability in the Context of Faith	146
Jesus as the Ultimate Example of Vulnerability	147
The Connection Between Vulnerability and Anxiety	148
Practical Ways to Embrace Vulnerability	149
How to Overcome Barriers to Vulnerability	150
The Role of Vulnerability in Relationships	151
Healing Through Vulnerability	152
God's Grace in Our Vulnerability	153
Practical Steps Toward Authentic Connection	154
Chapter 15: Healing Yourself by Helping Others	**155**
Understanding the Importance of Boundaries	157
Deeper Level Active Listening Techniques	158
Providing Scriptural Encouragement	159
The Message	160
Chapter 16: Your Beautiful Future	**163**

> *"Surrender to what is,
> let go of what was,
> and have faith in what will be."*
>
> ~ Sonia Ricotti ~

Introduction

It feels like it was only yesterday. That day, anxiety felt like a heavy, suffocating blanket, completely crushing my energy and spirit. I was crying in my car, and all I could think was, could my faith in God save me?

The cause stemmed from a series of circumstances: a failing business I was working 14-hour days, seven days a week, to save; the loss of my brother, sister, and mother within 18 months of each other; and the realization that I would have to relocate from a place I loved and didn't want to leave to a place I wasn't ready to move to. It felt like every moment I spent by myself was a fight against the feelings of anxiety, depression, and fear that kept coming up inside me until finally, it all hit me at once.

At that same moment, I realized I was suffering from severe burnout.

Surely, this wasn't God's plan for me.

You may have felt the same way, if not for the same reasons. As you've sat alone with those racing thoughts, you may have felt like your faith in God and your mental health were at odds with each other. No matter how strongly we, as Christians, believe in what we believe, the waves of worry can feel like they can't be beaten even with our faith in God.

It's only now, 8 years later, that I'm ready to share how I overcame this crippling anxiety and the depression that had me gripped in its claws. I wrote this book to help you cope with anxiety and learn about transforming fears through the sacred act of worship. It is possible to discover reserves of strength you never knew existed, even amidst your struggles, just like I did. This change from worry to worship offers hope and wholeness through the integration of faith, down-to-earth strategies, and mindful lifestyle changes.

This book is for those who are tired of oversimplified advice that doesn't fully acknowledge the complexities of anxiety, especially when it intersects with Christian faith. We will explore holistic solutions that respect your spiritual beliefs as well as your mental well being. You'll find some actionable steps to nurture emotional peace, deepen your relationship with God, and create sustainable healing.

To start, ask yourself: What has my anxiety been trying to teach me about my relationship with God and myself?

In these pages, I'll share personal experiences and the strategies that helped me heal physically, emotionally, and spiritually. You'll learn practices like:

- How to turn worry into worship through intentional prayer and scripture.

- Simple mindfulness techniques to calm your thoughts and focus on God's presence.

- Lifestyle shifts that integrate faith with mental health.

Today, one step you can take is to choose a Bible verse you love to repeat when you feel anxious. For me, that verse was John 14:27: *"Peace I leave with you; my peace I give you. I do not give to you as the world gives. Do not let your hearts be troubled and do not be afraid."* That verse became a lifeline in my darkest moments.

As someone who understands and has overcome the isolation and helplessness that long-term anxiety and depression can bring, I hope that this book will be helpful to you. Together, we'll explore holistic solutions that honor both your Christian values and your mental well-being. The aim is to put together actionable strategies in alignment with your spiritual path, nurturing emotional peace while deepening your relationship with God.

My personal experiences and the strategies are not a substitute for professional medical advice or therapy. Anxiety and depression can have complex causes that may require medical attention or therapeutic support. If you're under the care of a doctor or mental health professional, I encourage you to use the insights and practices shared here alongside your treatment plan if you find them appropriate. I've written this as a resource to inspire and support you as you create your own unique and personal path to healing.

So, what are the main struggles you will face? I know for me, my feelings of anxiety and depression seemed compounded by an overwhelming sense of feeling isolated or trapped. The strain of adult and business responsibilities exacerbated my feelings. I'm sure you can empathize with that. Life can feel like a dangerous balancing act between personal, professional, and spiritual obligations. What's needed is coherent guidance that resonates with both your deeply held beliefs and your personal experiences.

Receiving a diagnosis of anxiety or depression can be intimidating, particularly if traditional resources don't resonate with your personal experience. Perhaps you are seeking help that integrates your Christian beliefs with practical mental health practices, but the available information is general and not in-depth enough to address the intensity of your challenges.

It's perfectly understandable to want sustainable, long-term healing that doesn't compromise your faith. You're seeking not only emotional peace but also a deeper spiritual growth and connection to God that integrates psychological and lifestyle strategies while staying true to your faith. I want to meet you exactly where you are, with compassion, empathy, and respect for your experience.

You might feel unsure about how to tackle the changes needed for healing, especially if they seem overwhelming or out of reach. Maybe you're wondering how to blend modern mental health practices with the deeply rooted Christian faith you hold close. It's okay to feel that tension; it's normal. Instead of trying to figure it all out at once, focus on taking small, steady steps. Each one counts, no matter how minor it may seem, and they'll lead you closer to the peace and healing you're looking for.

I pray that if there's one thing I can do, it's to give you hope and grace-filled guidance so you can navigate these challenges. If you have experienced extreme trauma, such as abuse, please consider getting help from a therapist if you haven't already. The path to healing isn't always linear; in fact, it's more likely to be a squiggly path that loops back on itself while ideas and solutions integrate into your life. It's certainly not the same for everyone. I had to move outside the traditional box to start seeing improvements and eventually arrive where I'm at now. My aim is to empower you to heal yourself by giving you a toolkit that addresses emotional, physical, and spiritual well-being in a holistic manner.

In the beginning, keep in mind that the purpose of this book is to offer empathy and provide practical solutions for achieving freedom and serenity. There's no rush and no pressure to race through the process. I want you to find the understanding and validation you need, combined with simple solutions to change your life and put your anxiety behind you. It's time to learn how to turn worry into worship and feel the healing power of belief in God alongside Christian and self-healing practices flowing together naturally.

"How long, Lord? Will you forget me forever? How long will you hide your face from me?" (Psalm 13:1)

Similarly, Job faced overwhelming trials, leading to deep distress and questioning. In Job 19:13-20, Job feels abandoned by his family, friends, and community, compounding his emotional pain. However, Job's faith is shown through his conversations with God. These discussions offer great lessons in managing anxiety.

"He has alienated my family from me; my acquaintances are completely estranged from me. ... I am nothing but skin and bones; I have escaped only by the skin of my teeth." (Job 19:13, 20)

Scripture acknowledges that anxiety is normal, and even these biblical figures illustrate that. From their ancient stories come modern insights. Through the experiences of these faithful individuals, Christians can use them to better understand their emotional struggles.

It is important to understand the sources of anxiety from both a psychological and biblical perspective. Anxiety isn't an abstract feeling. It comes from internal and external pressures. It may come from personal insecurities or past trauma that occur internally, as well as the added pressures of modern life we put upon ourselves. It could be a result of external life events, societal expectations, or relational conflicts. Once you've identified these sources, you can then face your anxiety by learning why and how it affects you.

Prayer as a foundational tool to manage anxiety allows us to come into God's presence. By turning to prayer, you begin to bridge the gap between anxiety and faith, showing you that spiritual methods can fit alongside more traditional mental health healing protocols.

Studying biblical texts can help you better understand your struggles through a deeper understanding of scripture. This will make you have a stronger faith and relationship with God. By relating your experiences to those found in God's Word, you not only gain insight from the lives of others but will also find the internal strength and intuitive guidance you need to move beyond anxiety. This process of integrating your personal story with biblical truths can bring about healing and spiritual growth. In turn, it will help you to view anxiety through a faith-filled perspective.

By understanding where exactly the anxiety has taken hold in your life— whether in your thoughts, circumstances, or relationships—you can begin to address it. With God's help, you can take practical, intentional steps to manage these areas. Through prayer, scripture, and trust in God, you find will strength. Add psychological tools, and you create balance. This blended approach heals your mind, body, and spirit with God at the center.

Make it a habit of seeking God when you worry. Doing this helps you practice relying on Him for peace. This will ease your immediate fears. Actively nurturing your spiritual life feeds your soul. It gives you a sense of purpose and hope that goes beyond temporary emotions.

When you make your faith a main part of how you approach anxiety, you start to change your outlook. Instead of feeling like anxiety is impossible to overcome, you come to realize that it is an opportunity to get to know God better. This is a great chance to strengthen your trust in Him and experience His power at work in your life.

Exploring the Role of Scripture in Understanding Anxiety

The Bible contains stories of individuals whose faith faced many tests. These were the people who were afraid, who weren't sure, who had so much going on, and yet they found strength in their faith.

It allows you to view your anxiety in a spiritual light. It provides clarity and a sense of hope. Anxiety often comes from confusion and fear of what we don't know, but God's Word offers a way to minimize these worries.

For instance, consider verses like Philippians 4:6-7.

"Do not be anxious about anything, but in every situation, by prayer and petition, with thanksgiving, present your requests to God. And the peace of God, which transcends all understanding, will guard your hearts and your minds in Christ Jesus.."

This passage encourages you to bring everything to God in prayer. It is promising peace that surpasses understanding. When you immerse yourself in scripture during moments of anxiety, you anchor your mind and heart in truths that counter the lies and distortions anxiety can create. God's love for you is unwavering and unconditional. Everything He does is for your greater good, even when your path ahead seems uncertain.

The Bible provides you with helpful tools to tackle anxiety. Verses such as 2 Timothy 1:7 remind us that God has not given us a spirit of fear, but rather a spirit of power, love, and a sound mind.

"For the Spirit God gave us does not make us timid but gives us power, love, and self-discipline."

It can help you think differently about anxious thoughts if you take a moment to reflect on these truths. The scripture does not allow the fear to lead but instead asks you to put your trust in God's sovereignty and His strength.

Reading biblical passages and stories can help you find inspiration from those who have gone through similar challenges. David, for instance, frequently shared his fears with God in the Psalms while also continually expressing his trust in God's faithfulness. His example shows you that it's okay to acknowledge your fears while still holding on to the promises of God. Even Jesus, in His humanity, prayed fervently in the Garden of Gethsemane, showing you how important it is to turn to the Father in times of deep emotional distress. These stories remind you that God offers you guidance and comfort as you navigate your anxieties.

Ultimately, scripture points you toward a deeper reliance on God, even when anxiety feels overwhelming. It reminds you that you're not defined by your fears but by your identity as a beloved child of God. Through the Word, you can start to see anxiety differently—not as a barrier between you and God, but as a chance to get closer to Him. Through each prayer, reflection, and act of faith, you welcome His peace into your life, turning anxiety into the catalyst of deeper spiritual growth.

> *"You may not control all the events that happen to you, but you can decide not to be reduced by them."*
>
> ~ Maya Angelou ~

Chapter 1: Understanding Anxiety Through Faith

Taking a biblical view of anxiety can offer you a better understanding of what it means for you and how to handle it. The burden of everyday pressures can create intense worry, which can challenge your ability to maintain your faith. What if you use your anxiety as a chance to strengthen your connection with God and experience His power in your human limitations? When you change your mindset, you discover how Scripture acts as both a source of direction and support while presenting practical methods to manage anxiety that help strengthen your faith. Coming up, you'll learn how God and Scripture will provide you with the tools to confront your challenges directly.

Defining Anxiety in a Spiritual/Biblical Context

When you consider anxiety through a biblical lens, it really highlights how connected it is to your spiritual journey. Anxiety is a state of fear that disrupts your peace. For some, it might feel like a disconnect from God. This disruption, along with its accompanying feelings of guilt (especially for Christians), stems from the perception that anxiety is a sign of a lack of faith. It's possible to feel the guilt acutely, thinking that your struggles mean you're failing spiritually. But this is something that needs to be approached with self-compassion rather than judgment.

Fear and anxiety are universal human experiences that are directly addressed in the Bible. David, for instance, often revealed his fears and anxieties in Psalms. Despite being a man after God's own heart, even he had times when stress and worry got the better of him.

In Psalm 3, David expresses fear and trust while fleeing from his son Absalom. He acknowledges the many enemies against him but declares that God is his shield and deliverer.

"But you, Lord, are a shield around me, my glory, the One who lifts my head high." (Psalm 3:3)

In Psalm 13, David wrestles with feelings of abandonment and despair, yet ultimately reaffirms his trust in God's unfailing love.

"How long, Lord? Will you forget me forever? How long will you hide your face from me?" (Psalm 13:1)

Similarly, Job faced overwhelming trials, leading to deep distress and questioning. In Job 19:13-20, Job feels abandoned by his family, friends, and community, compounding his emotional pain. However, Job's faith is shown through his conversations with God. These discussions offer great lessons in managing anxiety.

"He has alienated my family from me; my acquaintances are completely estranged from me. ... I am nothing but skin and bones; I have escaped only by the skin of my teeth." (Job 19:13, 20)

Scripture acknowledges that anxiety is normal, and even these biblical figures illustrate that. From their ancient stories come modern insights. Through the experiences of these faithful individuals, Christians can use them to better understand their emotional struggles.

It is important to understand the sources of anxiety from both a psychological and biblical perspective. Anxiety isn't an abstract feeling. It comes from internal and external pressures. It may come from personal insecurities or past trauma that occur internally, as well as the added pressures of modern life we put upon ourselves. It could be a result of external life events, societal expectations, or relational conflicts. Once you've identified these sources, you can then face your anxiety by learning why and how it affects you.

Prayer as a foundational tool to manage anxiety allows us to come into God's presence. By turning to prayer, you begin to bridge the gap between anxiety and faith, showing you that spiritual methods can fit alongside more traditional mental health healing protocols.

Studying biblical texts can help you better understand your struggles through a deeper understanding of scripture. This will make you have a stronger faith and relationship with God. By relating your experiences to those found in God's Word, you not only gain insight from the lives of others but will also find the internal strength and intuitive guidance you need to move beyond anxiety. This process of integrating your personal story with biblical truths can bring about healing and spiritual growth. In turn, it will help you to view anxiety through a faith-filled perspective.

By understanding where exactly the anxiety has taken hold in your life—whether in your thoughts, circumstances, or relationships—you can begin to address it. With God's help, you can take practical, intentional steps to manage these areas. Through prayer, scripture, and trust in God, you find will strength. Add psychological tools, and you create balance. This blended approach heals your mind, body, and spirit with God at the center.

Make it a habit of seeking God when you worry. Doing this helps you practice relying on Him for peace. This will ease your immediate fears. Actively nurturing your spiritual life feeds your soul. It gives you a sense of purpose and hope that goes beyond temporary emotions.

When you make your faith a main part of how you approach anxiety, you start to change your outlook. Instead of feeling like anxiety is impossible to overcome, you come to realize that it is an opportunity to get to know God better. This is a great chance to strengthen your trust in Him and experience His power at work in your life.

Exploring the Role of Scripture in Understanding Anxiety

The Bible contains stories of individuals whose faith faced many tests. These were the people who were afraid, who weren't sure, who had so much going on, and yet they found strength in their faith. It allows you to view your anxiety in a spiritual light. It provides clarity and a sense of hope. Anxiety often comes from confusion and fear of what we don't know, but God's Word offers a way to minimize these worries.

For instance, consider verses like Philippians 4:6-7.

"Do not be anxious about anything, but in every situation, by prayer and petition, with thanksgiving, present your requests to God. And the peace of God, which transcends all understanding, will guard your hearts and your minds in Christ Jesus."

This passage encourages you to bring everything to God in prayer. It is promising peace that surpasses understanding. When you immerse yourself in scripture during moments of anxiety, you anchor your mind and heart in truths that counter the lies and distortions anxiety can create. God's love for you is unwavering and unconditional. Everything He does is for your greater good, even when your path ahead seems uncertain.

The Bible provides you with helpful tools to tackle anxiety. Verses such as 2 Timothy 1:7 remind us that God has not given us a spirit of fear, but rather a spirit of power, love, and a sound mind.

"For the Spirit God gave us does not make us timid but gives us power, love, and self-discipline."

It can help you think differently about anxious thoughts if you take a moment to reflect on these truths. The scripture does not allow the fear to lead but instead asks you to put your trust in God's sovereignty and His strength.

Reading biblical passages and stories can help you find inspiration from those who have gone through similar challenges. David, for instance, frequently shared his fears with God in the Psalms while also continually expressing his trust in God's faithfulness. His example shows you that it's okay to acknowledge your fears while still holding on to the promises of God.

Even Jesus, in His humanity, prayed fervently in the Garden of Gethsemane, showing you how important it is to turn to the Father in times of deep emotional distress. These stories remind you that God offers you guidance and comfort as you navigate your anxieties.

Ultimately, scripture points you toward a deeper reliance on God, even when anxiety feels overwhelming. It reminds you that you're not defined by your fears but by your identity as a beloved child of God. Through the Word, you can start to see anxiety differently—not as a barrier between you and God, but as a chance to get closer to Him.

Through each prayer, reflection, and act of faith, you welcome His peace into your life, turning anxiety into the catalyst of deeper spiritual growth.

Chapter 2: Trusting God in Stressful Times

Trusting God during stressful situations can be hard, even for us devout Christians. By showing Him that you are in faith, you begin letting go of some of your anxieties. This lets you trust your faith, which transcends your worries. When God and Jesus are with you, you don't have to be worried about anxiety burdening your shoulders. What if your heavy loads became lighter and you trusted that God's got it covered? Leaning on him allows you to explore a deeper relationship with Him and trust even more than you already do.

Building Trust through Prayer

Relying on God will help keep you grounded. This trust is a conscious decision on your part to lean into God's sovereignty. If you accept that God is in charge and stop micromanaging your life, you can start to let go. Once you accept this, you will feel at peace. Then you can pull back from your stress and realize that, even in chaos, there is divine order at work.

God's sovereignty provides a steady and unshakable truth in your life. If your anxiety has caused you to somewhat disconnect from Him, you need to relearn to trust in His greater plans. Know that He sees the end from the beginning. Understanding this aspect of God's character reassures you that nothing catches Him by surprise, and no worry you face is beyond His ability to handle.

Worship is a powerful tool that shifts your focus from worry to faith. In times of distress, it's easy to become consumed by what might go wrong or what is already falling apart. Worship, however, calls you to lift your gaze beyond your immediate circumstances. When we engage in worship, we declare God's greatness, recount His promises, and remind ourselves of His unwavering love. This act not only honors God but also redirects our mindset to the truth of His attributes—His power, authority, and compassion.

Through worship, we acknowledge that while our problems may be significant, they are not insurmountable for the Creator who holds the universe together. It changes our perspective, helping us to see our difficulties through the lens of God's omnipotence rather than the limitations of our human understanding. Worship becomes a refuge, a place where fears dissipate as we are enveloped by the assurance of God's presence.

At the heart of strengthening trust in God is prayer, a direct line of communication with our Creator. Prayer isn't just about asking for help; it's a spiritual exchange that transforms anxiety into trust. Imagine yourself confiding in Him, where His grace gently listens to every concern and lifts it away. Through prayer, we forge a connection with God that is intimate and revealing. It allows us to express our deepest fears and uncertainties, knowing that God listens and responds.

Engaging in open and honest communication with God means you are being transparent with yourself and Him. Nothing remains hidden. As you voice your anxieties and uncertainties, you'll feel much more peace and clarity. It's why you may turn to friends for help, as well as to God. As time goes on, this practice helps build a sense of confidence that God is not just paying attention to you but is also actively working to shape things for your best interests.

Establishing a regular practice of prayer strengthens your reliance on the divine. Building up your faith and trust in God will have a positive effect on anxiety. Creating a structured routine can make it easier to fit prayer into your everyday life. So, whether you set aside certain times during the day or use a phone app for reminders to pray, consistency is the key.

A healthy prayer life might begin small—perhaps with a simple morning prayer of gratitude or an evening rundown of the day's happenings offered up to God. As this discipline grows, so does our ability to rely on God. Each prayer adds to the foundation of our trust. As we commit to this path, we find that prayer becomes a natural first response rather than a desperate last resort.

Steps to Relinquish Control to God

Letting go of your fears and handing control over to God can start to change things for you. It's all about being aware of yourself, taking some practical steps, and finding spiritual support. What are the specific situations or areas of your life where you tend to want to control things? Anxiety often pops up when you feel the need to micromanage every little thing in your life. Think about those times when trying to control everything just ends up making you feel more stressed out. Recognizing these patterns lets you welcome God into those areas of your life.

Think about what it means to actually let go. Imagine holding your fears right there in your hands and then releasing them, trusting them to God's care. Why not try something physical? You could write down your worries on paper and then tear it up or burn it. It's a great way to show your trust in Him in a more tangible way. These simple actions help you lean more on God.

Another idea is to look to the scriptures to strengthen your trust with verses like Jeremiah 17:7-8.

"But blessed is the one who trusts in the Lord, whose confidence is in him. They will be like a tree planted by the water, that sends out its roots by the stream. It does not fear when heat comes; its leaves are always green."

It's an excellent reminder to hand over your worries to God and receive His peace in return. When you keep saying these words, they start to settle in your heart, slowly pushing out fear and bringing in a sense of calm confidence. Take a moment to feel God's presence with you. Remember, He's fully capable of taking on your burdens.

The uncertainty of life is all part of your spiritual journey. Life can be unpredictable, but when you embrace that reality, it helps to boost your faith. Proverbs 3:5-6 encourages you to put your trust in the Lord wholeheartedly, rather than just depending on your own understanding.

"Trust in the Lord with all your heart and lean not on your own understanding; in all your ways submit to him, and he will make your paths straight."

Ease up on self-inflicted pressure. You don't have to do everything by yourself. Instead, ask God for wisdom as you try to lighten your mental load.Try to develop simple habits that will support this way of thinking. Things like meditating on scripture, starting your day with gratitude, or even a couple moments at night to reflect on how you gave up control during the day can really make a difference in shifting your mind from worrying to trusting. Doing these regular practices helps you connect better with God and strengthens your faith.

Make prayer a key part of how you build trust. Talk to God in a way that feels personal and specific, sharing your fears and desires honestly. Journaling your prayers can be impactful. It gives you a chance to keep track of your thoughts and notice how God responds as time goes on. This practice will help you see things more clearly. It boosts your resilience as you notice how much you're growing spiritually.

It's up to you to come up with a personalized way to weave faith-based routines into your everyday life in a way that will minimize your anxiety. Try using tools like daily devotionals to share your feelings, define your dreams, and note what you're grateful for. If you would like one specifically created for anxiety, then you'll love *From Worry to Worship: A 52-Week Devotional Bible Study for Anxiety*. These habits help you get closer to God and feel more peaceful.

Integrating Daily Acts of Trust

You have a new opportunity each day to practice trust. There are many ways to strengthen your faith and trust in God when you're anxious. And that's why it's important to focus on small, intentional actions that help you let go when life seems overwhelming. Start small; make the choice to replace worry with prayer. When you wake up, instead of allowing your mind to start amplifying the things you're worrying about, take a moment to pray. When you do this simple thing, it brings God's care and reassurance into your day. It helps you shift your focus away from the things that might be dragging you down.

Choosing prayer over worry is more than a habit; it's a practice that builds spiritual confidence. By routinely pausing to pray whenever worry arises, you lighten your emotional load and strengthen your belief in God's ability to handle your challenges. Each intentional prayer deepens your faith, helping you trust in His power over your circumstances.

Daily and consistent acts of trust will lead to lasting change. When you build resilience against fear, you focus on Him through personal prayers and reflections. This is why it is helpful to meditate on scripture or to journal about His assurances (He will never leave you nor forsake you). These affirm your faith and become a truth inside of you even in uncertain times.

Including these ideas into your daily routine can help you stay calm and act like a shield against anxiety. As time passes, you'll begin to notice that God's support becomes clearer, giving you the confidence to face life's challenges head-on. It's important to notice and appreciate those little things in your day. Engaging in a conversation over coffee or immersing yourself in a breathtaking scene in nature are examples of such moments. These reminders of God being with us really help you lean on Him more and turn everyday moments into something special and spiritual.

Breath prayers are an excellent way to invite His calm into your life. They are easy; you silently concentrate on a single word or phrase as you inhale, usually one that symbolizes God's peace, such as "peace" or "Jesus." You then imagine releasing your fears or anxieties when you exhale, allowing them to leave your body. In addition to the calmness you'll feel after doing your breath prayers, this exercise strengthens your spiritual bond. It makes room for God's presence in your life. With each breath you take, you are completely giving your worries to God. When you hand over your worries to Him, you let go of those that are beyond your control. If you practice this simple technique regularly, you'll find it assists with mental clarity and brings a sense of spiritual peace.

These little habits will help create a solid base of trust and faith, keeping you steady during difficult times. Every choice you make, every prayer you say, and every moment of reflection helps you connect more deeply with God. When you take these steps, you're creating a well-rounded way to handle life's ups and downs, all while relying on God's steady support.

Group Prayer to Help with Anxiety

Meeting up with others to pray can really help boost our faith and trust in God. These get-togethers bring people closer to each other, helping to build a community rooted in the shared belief in a higher power's intentions. This can help you reduce your feelings of anxiety.

Joining others in prayer gives you the support you may not have experienced when trying to manage your anxiety by yourself. The right group will offer you both kindness and support. You'll have the chance to form close friendships with others, so you won't feel alone in what you're experiencing. It's beneficial to have people around when you're feeling vulnerable, especially those who understand what you're going through. This gives you that comforting feeling right when you really need it.

Group prayer boosts your spirits and can help with any feelings of isolation you might be experiencing. This communal praying experience draws people together. It's a wonderful reminder that support is all around you, even in difficult circumstances.

The sight of someone expressing complete confidence in God through prayer generates renewed enthusiasm in you to take part in this spiritual expression. We see in the communal power of belief how human resilience transforms into a shared strength across our shared identity. Seeing other people following divine direction, you find yourself drawn to build stronger faith, which brings you closer to Him.

When you come together with others looking for divine guidance, your spiritual roots really thrive, growing stronger through the shared experience. This collective search for God's presence reassures you that He is always near, offering comfort and strengthening the bond of faith between you and others.

At first, stepping into group prayer might feel intimidating, or you might feel self-conscious, but the welcoming atmosphere soon eases those fears. In these gatherings, there is no judgment. Authenticity is very much encouraged. This openness invites you to bring your true self to the table, finding peace in your honest connection with God and fellow Christians.

The connections made in group prayer often extend beyond the prayer time itself. The support you receive and offer continues to nourish you long after the "Amen." These bonds inspire you to reach out in times of need and offer prayer support outside of scheduled gatherings, showing you that faith is a shared experience, strengthened through mutual belief and community.

Group prayer blends solitude and community, giving you space for personal reflection while maintaining the power of collective support. It creates an environment ripe for spiritual renewal, refreshing your soul and mind when facing tough times.

When you join hands in prayer, whether physically or through online platforms, you connect with others across different walks of life. The diversity of experiences and perspectives adds richness to your prayer, blending different stories into one unified expression of faith. In these moments, the barriers of distance and difference fade, replaced by a shared pursuit of divine comfort and understanding.

Wrapping Up

In this chapter, you've been taught how to let go of your fears and trust in God. For peace and balance in a chaotic world, you have to let go of the need to control everything. Prayer helps you remember that God hears your concerns. Regular practice of prayer, worship, and Bible reading strengthens this belief. These habits help shift your focus from fear to trust. When you start incorporating these strategies, you're creating a blend of your faith with practical mental health practices that create holistic healing.

> *"The greatest glory in living*
> *lies not in never falling,*
> *but in rising every time we fall."*
>
> ~ Nelson Mandela ~

Chapter 3: Integrating Prayer with Mental Health Tools

Bringing together prayer and mental health tools is a wonderful way to connect your faith with your emotional well-being. By blending these elements, you can find your way through the overwhelming anxiety in a manner that feels easy and reassuring. Prayer, with its rich spiritual practices, provides both comfort and a chance for true reflection and understanding. When paired with structured psychological tools, it serves as a helpful link between your beliefs and the practical steps needed to manage anxious thoughts.

Combining Prayer with Cognitive Behavioral Techniques

You can start managing anxiety by combining prayer with cognitive-behavioral techniques. This is crucial for Christians seeking faith-centered approaches to find relief from anxiety. When you bring these practices into your daily routine, you'll discover you feel more peace, even when things get a bit stressful.

Cognitive Behavioral Therapy, or CBT, is a form of therapy that helps you spot and shift the negative thoughts and behaviors that might be causing you emotional stress. It's all about how your thoughts, feelings, and behaviors are linked together. If you start to notice and change these patterns, you might find that your emotional well-being begins to improve.

CBT teaches practical stress and mental health problem-solving methods while assisting you to establish clear objectives. In CBT you establish goals which transform large obstacles into manageable smaller tasks. Any goal you set needs to be specific, measurable, and about practical changes.

For example, you might set goals such as:

- Challenge one negative thought each day by replacing it with a positive or neutral one.

- Practice deep breathing exercises once a day.
- Schedule one self-care activity each week.
- Choose a time for worry each day to limit how long you spend in an anxious state.

Ideas like these will help you work towards positive outcomes and measure your progress as you progress.

To manage anxiety with CBT, first identify the negative thoughts that stress triggers. If you find yourself thinking in stressful ways, read verses from the Bible instead. For example, when you start to get an anxious feeling, you might think of the Philippians 4:6-7 verse that was previously shared. This passage tells you to bring your worries to God in prayer, knowing that His peace will guard your heart and mind.

When anxiety creeps in, challenge those worries with faith. Instead of letting fear take control, counteract it with Scripture and prayer. God's word can help you feel grounded, like in Isaiah 41:10, where He promises to strengthen and uphold you. Switching out those anxious thoughts for God's Word helps you shift your focus from fear to faith.

Reframing those fearful thoughts is a key aspect of CBT. So, when you catch yourself thinking, "I'm not good enough," try swapping that out for the passage in Romans 8:1. *"Therefore, there is now no condemnation for those who are in Christ Jesus, because through Christ Jesus the law of the Spirit who gives life has set you free from the law of sin and death."* This helps shift your mindset from a place of fear to a place of faith in God's love.

Besides changing how you think, mindfulness practices can help you stay focused on what's happening right now. When you start feeling anxious, try to shift your focus to God's presence by taking a moment for some quiet reflection. By centering your mind on Him, you can relax a little knowing that He is with you through every anxious thought.

CBT helps you build up your coping skills. Also, adopting practices like gratitude and worship can help you manage stress and look at anxious situations in a new light. When you take a moment to thank God for what

He provides and worship Him during tough times, it helps keep your faith strong. This mindset can make dealing with anxiety feel a bit easier.

Begin by using prayer to help you identify and understand your negative thought patterns. Take a moment to focus on the thoughts that stir up anxiety. Sometimes, these thoughts can get a bit overwhelming if you don't keep an eye on them. This can end up leading to a narrative that affects how you feel emotionally. As you pray, welcome divine insight into your journey of self-reflection. Seek clarity to uncover the underlying reasons for your concerns. This transforms quiet reflection into a lively chat with God, guiding you to discover what might spark anxiety—be it a certain situation, a relationship, or an inner fear.

After you've spotted these negative patterns, the next step is to gently challenge them through prayer. Cognitive-behavioral strategies blend beautifully with your spiritual practices. Scripture can be a wonderful companion in transforming negative thoughts. When anxiety whispers that you're not enough or that disaster looms, gently counter those thoughts with verses that speak of peace and divine purpose. The Bible invites you to let go of anxiety and share your requests with God through prayer. Remember the Philippians 4:6-7 verse from earlier?

"Do not be anxious about anything; but in every situation, by prayer and petition, with thanksgiving, present your requests to God. And the peace of God, which transcends all understanding, will guard your hearts and your minds in Christ Jesus."

Use these words as your guiding mantra. Say them during stressful times to help redirect your focus. This scriptural engagement helps anchor your mind in truth and shifts your thinking from fear to faith.

As you embrace this approach, think about incorporating visualization during prayer to enhance its soothing impact. Visualization creates lovely mental images of peace and safety, bringing a sense of relief from distressing thoughts. Picture yourself putting your worries in a basket and envisioning God gently taking that basket away. Imagine calm settings—a soothing garden or a gentle ocean—filled with a feeling of comfort and a touch of the divine. This mental imagery takes you away from anxious thoughts and brings you into a peaceful space, reminding you that you can find calm with God's support.

Another wonderful practice involves asking questions with a prayerful heart. This can be a beneficial way to ease anxiety by concentrating on solutions instead of problems. While praying, consider asking yourself, "What am I really afraid of?" or "What is God's perspective on this situation?" These questions encourage you to engage in deeper thinking, which can break down the hold that anxiety has on you. It helps you focus on finding real solutions instead of getting caught up in problems.

By regularly including thoughtful questioning in your prayer routine, you can engage in cognitive restructuring, which is an important part of cognitive-behavioral therapy. This practice is an excellent way to build resilience against anxiety. It encourages you to look for wisdom beyond your immediate feelings, helping you develop a balanced perspective when facing those unsettling emotions or situations.

Regularly blending prayer with cognitive-behavioral techniques offers a wonderful way to support both your spiritual and mental well-being. This way, you can focus on your spiritual values as you navigate your healing journey, making it easier to deal with anxiety and find a lasting sense of happiness and tranquility.

Understanding and Confronting Spiritual Warfare

Dealing with anxiety and mental health can be difficult, especially when spiritual warfare comes into play. You may find your worries and fears becoming more acute, or your peace starts slipping away. These battles are more than just emotional or mental; they feel like an attack on your faith and your ability to place your trust in God. Anxiety can lead you into mental loops of doubt that leave you wondering if you're actually supported or loved.

Spiritual warfare can cloud the truth of who you are in Christ. The enemy, when he whispers things like 'You're not enough' or 'God doesn't care,' leaves you feeling defeated before you even start. The positive news is that when the battle is too heavy, God promises to give us strength.

Identifying the spiritual warfare strategies from the dark that lead to anxiety is an important first step in preparing yourself to face them. Scripture frequently addresses fear and doubt as challenges faced by

Christians. Understanding these tactics of darkness is crucial. Ephesians 6 offers a glimpse into how these spiritual strategies come to life, indicating that fear and doubt can chip away at your peace, resulting in anxiety.

Recognizing these dark spiritual influences is like discovering the forces that have infiltrated your mind. When you notice fear and doubt, as mentioned in scripture, you can start to see your experiences in a spiritual light. This helps you focus on healing more effectively. Think about how these elements play a role in your life and the impact they have on your mental state.

Once you see the spiritual warfare strategies at work, connect with practices that uplift and safeguard you both mentally and emotionally. The Armor of God, mentioned in Ephesians 6:13-18, is vital in this context. The Armor of God includes truth, righteousness, peace, faith, salvation, prayer, and the Word of God. If you don't use these tools, you are vulnerable to spiritual attacks. By embracing them, you're acknowledging their significance and actively utilizing them to uplift your mind and spirit.

This armor helps you bring these spiritual tools to your daily life. So, for example, in knowing the truth, you're remembering what you know about God's love as you fight against the lies of fear and doubt.

Righteousness keeps your heart safe, inspiring actions and thoughts that resonate with your beliefs.

Peace, as part of this armor, serves as a shield against anxiety, helping you discover calm where there was once unrest.

Faith boosts your defenses, helping you remember the bigger picture and the promises that bring comfort, which lessens the hold of fear and doubt.

The key is to cling to His truth, to battle with His Word, and to choose to believe that you will never be abandoned.

Designing a Prayer Routine for Mental Well-Being

To create a prayer routine that strengthens your mental well-being, set a regular daily time for your prayers. Having a schedule adds a beneficial touch of calm to your day. Pick a special time when you feel the most reflective. Stick to consistent times. This is your personal commitment to your spiritual growth and mental well-being.

There are different ways to pray that can help you to heal. Meditative prayer can really be calming, allowing you to feel closer to God and find some peace. Intercessory prayer is all about praying for others. It will help you take your mind off your own worries. It's a really good way to build empathy and feel more connected to those around you. You can also combine prayer with visualization, as imagination and mental imagery can aid in the integration of healing. This is known as prayerful imagery.

Writing in a journal while you pray can be a useful addition to your routine. Putting your prayers and reflections into writing helps bring clarity, allowing you to better comprehend your emotions and chart your personal growth. The small victories you'll uncover will really help your progress. These are the moments when you notice an easing of your anxious thoughts or a slight increase in calmness. They definitely keep you inspired as you work through your healing journey.

For a lot of people, mixing these parts of life can feel a bit shaky at first. It's pretty common to have questions about how to balance spiritual and psychological methods. But as you keep integrating these practices into your everyday routine, you'll find yourself naturally developing habits that blend both areas. Just be patient and open, and you'll find what works for you.

Reflections and Takeaways

In this chapter, you've learned how to use cognitive behavioral techniques with prayer as a powerful way to deal with anxiety if you're seeking a faith-based approach. Praying to counteract negative thought patterns allows you to gain Christian insight into your self-reflection process. This transforms passive moments into an active dialogue with God. By integrating scripture to counteract anxious thoughts, you create a foundation of peace that helps you view challenges through the lens of faith.

Visualizing peace and safety during prayer takes your mind away from anxiety-driven scenarios, reminding you that calm is within reach through God's support. This holistic approach nurtures both your spiritual and mental well-being, aligning your inner struggles with your spiritual beliefs.

Keep in mind that this practice is an ongoing commitment. Setting up a daily routine where prayer and therapeutic techniques work together supports this integrative method, gradually changing the way you handle stressors. This approach offers more than just a quick fix; it helps develop mental resilience and brings you back to God frequently.

As you continue to add these habits into your routine, you're creating a method that honors your spiritual path and the practical steps necessary to care for your mental health. Keep trying out what feels right for you and stay open to finding those deeper links between your faith and how you feel mentally.

"The tough times, the days when you're just a ball on the floor — they'll pass. You're playing the long game, and life is totally worth it."

~ Sarah Silverman ~

Chapter 4: Mindfulness and Christian Practices

It is possible to build emotional stability by practicing mindfulness along with Christian practices. Together, these two practices can offer a more effective approach to seeking a more God-centered source of peace and meaning. Mindfulness is about bringing your awareness to the present moment. It is consistent with Christian beliefs. At it's core, mindfulness keeps your present, attentive, and aware. It is the embodiment of Psalm 46:10, *"Be still, and know that I am God."*

In this chapter, you will get to know how to include mindfulness in your Christian practices. Both can help you cope with stress and anxiety more meaningfully and comfortingly. Well-being isn't just about taking care of the mind; it's also about nurturing the spirit. Mindfulness offers several techniques to help you along the way.

Mindfulness Exercises with a Christian Focus

Mindfulness is a way to quiet your heart and draw closer to God. Mindfulness exercises that focus on His presence and His Word reduce stress and restore your daily life with His peace and guidance. I've put together some faith-based practices that enable greater spiritual bonds with Him.

Breath Awareness

Breath awareness can be a really calming tool when anxiety hits. By focusing on your breath, you can ground yourself and bring your mind back to the present moment. It works so well with Christian meditation or prayer, connecting you with God's word while helping you find that inner stillness. Just inhale peace and God's love and exhale worry and tension.

It's a simple practice that can help quiet those racing thoughts and bring some calm into the chaos. You can try this before reading scripture or during your morning devotions. Don't worry about getting it perfect; just let it help guide you to a place of peace.

Body Scanning

Another practice that works well is body scan meditation, where you tune into how your body feels. While praying, close your eyes and slowly shift your focus through each part of your body, from your toes all the way up to your head. Pay attention to any tension you're holding and consciously let it go, inviting God's healing into your body. It helps you become more aware of how your emotions show up physically, and it's an amazing way to appreciate how perfectly God made you. With time, this practice can help you better understand what you need and how you're feeling.

Gratitude Journal

Keeping a gratitude journal is a lovely way to invite mindfulness into your daily routine. It helps shift your focus from anxiety to appreciation, and it helps you notice all the blessings around you.

Be grateful for three things at first, then add more as it becomes a habit. It's an effortless but powerful way to nurture positive emotions and draw closer to God. And when you look back at your entries, you can see how faithful He's been during tough times, helping you grow in gratitude.

Spending Time in Nature

Nature walks are another excellent way to engage with the world around you and grow spiritually. Step outside for a walk or just sit in your garden. Make time to connect with nature by walking barefoot. It's important to stay in the present moment and take in the sights, sounds, and smells of nature. When you find yourself slipping back into anxious thoughts, receive everything around you with all of your senses and breathe.

The earth is God's handiwork and His presence everywhere. It's a relaxing way to clear your mind and get away from the busyness of your life. You can also use the verses from Psalms as prompts to connect with both nature and God.

Incorporating these mindfulness practices into your life doesn't have to be overwhelming. Start small. Pick one practice, let it grow, and add more when you're ready. Each of these techniques is like a tool to help you navigate life's challenges and bring more peace and stability. They blend so well with your Christianity as they offer practical ways to handle stress, anxiety, or fear. By doing this, you're not just taking care of your mental health but also strengthening your relationship with God.

Creating a Holy Space for Meditation

Unlike the meditation in other religions, such as Buddhism, Christian meditation is based on filling the mind with thoughts about the Bible and Christian devotions. Creating a personal holy space for meditation is a powerful way to deepen your spiritual practice and find emotional peace. It's a special place where you can focus on connecting with God away from the distractions of everyday life. Having a dedicated space can make it easier to engage in meaningful prayer and reflection, especially when you're dealing with anxiety, worry, or depression.

First, find a place that you feel is peaceful and quiet. It should be a little part of your world where you can tune out distractions and the stress of your day. It might be a spare room, a cozy corner, or even a quiet spot in your garden. The trick is to pick a place where you feel safe and peaceful—a place where you can focus more deeply when you pray and meditate. Many people find that places with natural light or a sense of privacy create a calming atmosphere.

Once you've found your spot, it's time to make it your own. You can add symbolic elements such as candles and a cross to represent hope and faith, and your Bible can serve as a reminder of your beliefs. These symbols will help focus your thoughts during your meditation. You can also add anything else that will help you connect to God.

Don't forget about the power of sound in your meditation space. Soft, calming sounds like running water or wind chimes can help quiet the noise in your mind, especially when you're feeling anxious. You can create an atmosphere of peace and sacredness during your meditation time, Bible study, or prayer by playing worship music, instrumental hymns, or soft classical music. These sounds aren't just calming, but they remind you of God's comfort and love. If you love nature, sounds like ocean waves or rustling leaves can help you feel more grounded in your faith.

Before you begin each meditation session, take a moment to set your intentions. Think about what you want to achieve—whether it's peace, guidance, strength, or gratitude. Aligning your heart with God's will brings clarity and direction to your time of reflection, making it more meaningful. Setting intentions helps you stay focused, grounded, and open to God's guidance. It also encourages emotional awareness and self-reflection, helping you understand your feelings and move toward healing.

Getting into a meditative state involves a series of steps that can vary slightly depending on the type of meditation you are doing, but here's a simple and common process to guide you:

1. Move into Your Quiet Space

Choose a space that's quiet and free from distractions. This helps create a calm environment where you can focus and relax.

2. Sit Comfortably

You don't need to sit in any special posture, but it's important to find a position that feels comfortable for you. You can sit cross-legged on the floor, on a cushion, or in a chair with your feet flat on the ground. The key is to sit with your back straight but not tense, allowing your body to relax.

3. Close Your Eyes

Gently close your eyes to minimize distractions. If that feels uncomfortable, you can keep them slightly open and focus on a point in front of you. An eye mask can be helpful to keep light out.

4. Focus on Your Breath

Pay attention to your breathing. Take slow, deep breaths, inhaling deeply through your nose and exhaling through your mouth. Focus on the sensation of your breath as it enters and leaves your body. This helps shift your focus away from daily thoughts and into the present moment.

5. Let Go of Distractions

As you meditate, your mind will naturally wander. This is normal. When thoughts pop up, simply acknowledge them without judgment and gently bring your focus back to your breath. The goal isn't to stop thinking altogether but to notice when your mind has wandered and return to your breath.

6. Use a Mantra or Affirmation (Optional)

Some people find it helpful to repeat a word or phrase (a mantra or affirmation) to help stay focused. It could be something simple like "peace," "calm," or even a spiritual phrase like "I am loved" or "God is with me." This repetition can act as a grounding tool, helping you return to the present moment when distractions arise.

7. Observe Your Body

As you settle into the rhythm of your breath, gently bring your awareness to your body. Check in with how it feels. You can do a mental scan, starting from your toes and moving up to your head, relaxing each area of your body. If you notice any tension, try to release it with each breath.

8. Stay Present

The longer you meditate, the easier it becomes to enter a state of deep relaxation. You might feel a sense of peace or detachment from daily concerns. Stay in this peaceful state for as long as feels comfortable, whether that's for a few minutes or longer.

9. Gradually End the Meditation

When you're ready to finish, begin to bring your awareness back to the room. Gently wiggle your fingers and toes, stretch your body, and slowly open your eyes. Take a moment to reflect on how you feel and express gratitude for the time you took to meditate.

By making space for growth and spiritual connection, you invite God to lead you toward greater wellness and peace. Daily meditation can make a massive difference in your anxiety levels. It's well known to be incredibly helpful in inducing a state of calm.

Integration of Mindful Breathing with Christian Practice

A lot of us Christians look to our faith for comfort. Because of this, we need practical ways to deal with the stress and anxiety of the day. An effective way to release tension is to practice mindful breathing every day. It's a straightforward and effective method to help your body and spirit find more balance, and it can bring you closer to God.

Shallow breathing is a typical symptom of physical anxiety and stress. When we feel anxious, our bodies go into fight or flight, which involves a set of physiological changes, including rapid and shallow breathing. Here's why shallow breathing occurs during anxiety:

Increased Sympathetic Nervous System Activity: When we experience anxiety, it activates the sympathetic nervous system, or "stress response." This system gets the body ready for a perceived threat by raising the heart rate, the blood pressure, and the breathing rate.

Focus on the Threat: When we are anxious, we tend to direct our focus toward the perceived threat, forgetting our natural breathing patterns.

Hyperventilation: Extreme anxiety or panic attacks can lead to too much deep breathing, causing hyperventilation, which can make you feel dizzy, lightheaded, and leave you tingling.

Shallow breathing can exacerbate anxiety symptoms in several ways:

Reduced Oxygen Intake: With shallow breaths, you aren't getting enough oxygen into your body, and so you can feel lightheaded or dizzy and fatigued.

Increased Carbon Dioxide Levels: If you are shallow breathing, you can build up carbon dioxide in the bloodstream, which can make you feel like you can't breathe. This can cause panic.

Reinforcing the Anxiety Cycle: The physical discomfort caused by shallow breathing can further increase anxiety levels, creating a vicious cycle.

The solution is mindful breathing. Mindful breathing comes down to being in the moment and noticing every breath you take. Just being aware of this can really help clear your mind and get your heart ready for a chat with God. To do this, you begin your prayer by tuning into your breath—inhale deeply, feeling the air fill your lungs, and then gently blowing it out. Repeat for five minutes or so, or until you start to relax. This practice can help you let go of worries, allowing your prayers to become more centered and meaningful.

During prayer or meditation, mindful breathing will help you stay focused. If your mind starts to drift, just gently return your focus to your breath. As you breathe, you might also feel some areas of tension in your body. As you are breathing in, invite peace into your life; as you breathe out, release the stress and worries that weigh you down. As time goes on, this simple practice can help you discover those little moments of peace in the midst of your anxiety.

To deepen your connection with God, you can add passages from the Bible to your breathing practice. As you breathe in, silently say a verse that brings you peace, like *"Be still and know that I am God"* (Psalm 46:10). As you breathe out, let the words integrate into your subconscious. This can help you stay grounded and fill your mind with God's word, which brings both spiritual and emotional healing.

Mindful breathing is also beneficial for your body. The more you practice, the better your body gets at absorbing oxygen, which helps you feel more energized. It also lowers your body's stress responses, like heart rate and blood pressure. Your body benefits from the calm you create in your mind.

If you struggle with anxiety or depression, mindful breathing can offer some relief. It's a tool you can use when emotions feel overwhelming. Start with just a few minutes a day. Slowly build it into your routine as you get more comfortable. Don't rush it—this is something you can grow into, not a quick fix.

As you continue to practice mindful breathing, it'll become something natural, something you do without thinking. Whether you're praying or just sitting in silence, it will be there to support you in your spiritual journey. It teaches you patience and gentleness, which are at the heart of the Christian faith and bring lasting healing.

Mindful breathing helps you relax and also clears space inside you where God can speak to you. This quote from Isaiah's might be helpful: *"Those who hope in the Lord will renew their strength."* (Isaiah 40:31). Through mindful breathing, that renewal becomes real in your life.

For busy people—whether you're working, parenting, or caring for others—it can be challenging to find time for stillness. Just a few minutes here and there can make a big difference to your anxiety! Learn to find those small, quiet moments throughout your day and appreciate the importance of nurturing your mind, body, and soul.

Mindful breathing is a lifestyle of purpose, faith, and peace in all you do.

Faith-Focused Reflection through Mindfulness

Mindful reflection can be a helpful tool for Christians who want to grow closer to God while dealing with emotions like anxiety and depression. Taking a moment to reflect on your daily experiences helps you become more aware of how God is working in your life. It helps you be more thankful that He is in your life.

When you set aside time to reflect, you're not just going through the motions; you're focusing on the little moments that show God's guidance. Think about an unexpected blessing, like a friendly conversation with a stranger or a problem that suddenly gets solved. Those moments in your life show how much God cares for you. Thinking about them really brings a sense of comfort and gratitude, doesn't it? Taking a moment to reflect mindfully helps you catch those little blessings that might otherwise go unnoticed. Similarly, feeling grateful can really boost your faith and emotional balance, along with reducing your feelings of anxiety.

Journaling is a straightforward and enjoyable way to add some mindful reflection to your Christian life. Writing down your thoughts and experiences helps you see just how much you've changed and grown over time. Your journal becomes a personal record of your spiritual progress. You can explore your feelings honestly and track your progress. It's also an exceptional way to spot patterns and see how God has been at work in your life. Journaling is like having a map to guide you and a mirror to reflect on how far you've come.

You can also deepen your practice by combining mindfulness with contemplative prayer. This type of prayer is all about quieting your mind and heart to really listen to God. By taking a break from distractions and being still, you make space to hear His guidance. Remember to create space during your prayers for His answers. You can do this by going into silence in between your prayers. This can be especially helpful if you're struggling with anxiety or depression because it allows you to surrender your worries to God and trust that He has a plan for you. It can reduce that feeling of overwhelm and help you feel more relaxed and grounded in His love.

Another excellent way to practice mindful reflection is by connecting with other Christians. They should be Christians who share your values. Being part of a community gives you the chance to swap insights and learn from each other's stories. Sharing these moments is bound to make you feel more connected, especially if you've been feeling a bit isolated. They let you know that you're not facing your struggles by yourself and that the wisdom of Christ is there to help guide you.

It's perfectly fine to take your time to try different things on your path to healing. Don't pressure yourself to have it all figured out right away. The aim is to be with God in the moment.

Start small by setting aside a few minutes each day for reflection. Whatever you decide to do—journal, pray, or reflect with friends—the important thing is to keep at it regularly. You can build and expand your practice as you feel led to. Don't be afraid to try new methods and see what is most meaningful to you. Mindfulness is personal, so take the time to find what works for you.

Adding mindful reflection to your daily routine can lead to emotional peace and a richer spiritual connection. When you create room for awareness and gratitude, you invite the opportunity to experience God's love in fresh and impactful ways. This practice is a lovely way to heal emotionally while growing in faith.

The "Faith Jar" for Moments of Anxiety

Sometimes anxiety sneaks in unannounced and catches you unawares. Your heart starts thumping, and your brain races at a mile a minute. These are the times that something as simple as a 'Faith Jar' might come in handy. It's such an uncomplicated thing to have around. It can offer comfort and focus when you need it most.

Here's how it works. Get an empty jar, bowl, or box, whatever you have lying around. Then write out some Bible verses, positive words, or promises of God to you on small pieces of paper. You could include verses like Lamentations 3:22-23.

"Because of the Lord's great love we are not consumed, for his compassions never fail. They are new every morning; great is your faithfulness." or Psalm 94:19 *"When anxiety was great within me, your consolation brought me joy."*

If a certain message from God has resonated with you during a tough time, write that down, too.

I started my own faith jar when I felt completely overwhelmed. At first, it felt a little odd, almost too simple to be of any use. But one night, after a particularly rough day, I grabbed a slip of paper from the jar. It was a verse I had jotted down weeks earlier—Matthew 11:28: *"Come to me, all who are weary and burdened, and I will give you rest."* That made me tear up. I sat there, holding the verse, feeling as if those words were a gentle whisper from God just for me.

What is beautiful about the Faith Jar is that it is personal. Your own handwriting, your favorite scriptures, and God's presence fill it. Having a little slip of paper to pull out and hold onto can be really comforting, especially when your thoughts feel all over the place and it's difficult to catch your breath. It's a useful tool for regaining focus when anxiety overwhelms you. It's a simple act, but one that creates space to pause and breathe.

Living the Lesson

The more you incorporate mindfulness in your spiritual practice, the more you will actually connect with God and have the emotional balance you want. Mindful breathing, keeping a gratitude journal, and taking a simple walk in nature... all of these activities can be the wonderful moments that feed your soul and your mind. These practices aren't meant to take the place of prayer or worship but to add something extra, giving you fresh ways to find peace and draw closer to God. Whether you're in your quiet space or just pausing for a moment in the middle of a busy day, these simple moments of mindfulness can bring healing and growth.

Just take it slowly, adding what feels right for your current situation. It could be beginning your day with a few mindful breaths or ending it by writing down something you're grateful for. No matter what you choose, I hope these practices help you develop a deeper and more peaceful connection with yourself and your faith. With that balance, you'll find the strength to face whatever life brings because God's love and strength are with you every step of the way.

*"You don't have to control your
thoughts. You just have to
stop letting them control you."*

~ Dan Millman ~

Chapter 5: Overcoming Anxiety with Actionable Steps

It's totally normal to feel overwhelmed by anxiety with everything going on around us, but what if you could begin to regain control, step by step? To start managing anxiety, focus on the little choices that change your perspective and bring you calm instead of just trying to eliminate it altogether.

In this chapter, you'll learn some straightforward but effective strategies that can really help you manage anxiety. When you make a few small changes, you'll begin to see a calmer, more balanced version of yourself.

Developing a Daily Anxiety Management Plan

Managing anxiety can be a lot more manageable than it seems. The best place to begin is by identifying the situations or thoughts that create your anxiety. When you understand what triggers you, you're in a great spot to tackle them directly. Think of each trigger like a clue in a puzzle. By identifying these moments, you can start preparing for them in a way that helps lessen their impact. It might help to keep a diary of this or a simple list—write down what's happening, what leads up to it, and how you feel during and after. It's not enough to just be aware of your anxiety; you need to take charge of your mental health and actively manage it.

Next, it's important to set small, realistic goals. You don't need to change everything at once; just focus on making steady, manageable progress. How about giving deep breathing a go for just five minutes today? Or you could choose to enjoy one meal at a slow pace with full awareness of the food you're eating. Let's celebrate these small wins! They boost your confidence and keep you focused on the bigger goals ahead.

Putting together an easy daily routine that includes some relaxation techniques is important. You don't have to change everything about your life; just pick one or two calming practices that really speak to you, like prayer, meditation, yoga, or even a slow walk in nature or after a meal. We're aiming for consistency. Having those little pockets of peace throughout your day really helps cut down on stress and brings a sense of stability. Imagine it as setting up important dates with yourself. Use these moments to take a breather and get back in touch with emotions.

It's also a good idea to check in with yourself regularly. Set aside a few minutes each week, maybe Sunday after church or Monday morning, to reflect on how things are going. What worked well? Did something new pop up? How are your anxiety levels? These check-ins help you adjust your plan if needed and give you a chance to celebrate the progress you've made. Plus, looking back at how far you've come can be really encouraging!

As you build your anxiety plan, don't forget to include your faith. For Christians, the plan is even stronger when it combines your relationship with God and Jesus with ways to deal with mental health issues. Plan your day so that you have time for Bible reading, prayer, or devotionals. It's a wonderful idea to include devotionals like From Worry to Worship: A 52-Week Devotional Bible Study for Anxiety that tackle fear and anxiety in your daily routine. They can help you stay focused on finding God's peace in your life. Reading parts of the Bible that talk about peace and strength will help you stay grounded and feel better.

For those of you juggling busy lives, remember that it's okay to make things fit your schedule. You don't need long, uninterrupted sessions—small moments of calm can add up. Take a deep breath, say a quick prayer, or find something to be grateful for. These quiet moments throughout your busy day can help you refocus and calm your mind.

Be patient. Your emotions are complex and your anxiety may take time to fade. It's perfectly fine to experience setbacks. Be kind to yourself and treat yourself like you would treat your best friend. Tackle things one step at a time. Making progress, even if it takes time, is still a step forward. Continue to rely on your faith to remain strong and progress, trusting that God is by your side every step of the way.

How to Release Trapped Emotions and Rewire Your Belief System

Recognizing and clearing negative emotions and self-beliefs starts with awareness. When you trigger a feeling of frustration, sadness, or anxiety, take the time to find out what's behind it while the feeling is still fresh. Ask yourself: What belief is behind this emotion? Often, subconscious thoughts such as I'm not good enough or I don't deserve love are shaping your reactions. You may not even realize it. Journaling is the best practice for bringing your subconscious patterns into your awareness. You'll likely need to go a few layers deeper than your initial thoughts about a trigger.

Once you've identified the underlying belief, you need to challenge its truth. Byron Katie's "The Work" offers a simple method to do this. Byron's method is in-depth and well worth studying, but here are the basics. Ask yourself:

- Is this belief absolutely true? and
- Who would I be without this thought?

The negative belief you hold will prove less concrete than you originally thought. The belief exists mostly as a narrative you have repeatedly told yourself. When we exchange our old thinking with new empowering ideas like I am worthy of love and respect, we start to change the present emotional patterns.

Finally, release and clear the emotion tied to the belief using either breathwork, EFT (tapping), or EMDR.

Using Therapeutic Breathwork for Immediate Relief

Earlier, we discussed mindful breathing. It's a very simple form of breathwork. In this section, you'll learn more advanced breathing techniques. These are more specific ways to heal from anxiety. By learning to manage your breathing, you give yourself a way to calm your mind and body when things feel overwhelming. It's something you can use in your daily life, whether you're facing a tough situation or just trying to create a little more calmness in your routine. It was one of the most valuable tools I used when healing from anxiety.

Breathwork: God's Gift for Healing Anxiety

In the beginning, when the earth was formless and void, the Spirit of God, the Ruach Elohim, hovered over the waters. This breath of God brought order from chaos. It created life from emptiness. Later, as Scripture tells us, God formed man from the dust of the ground and *"breathed into his nostrils the breath of life"* (Genesis 2:7). Your breath marks you as connected to your Creator. You are sustained moment by moment by His provision.

Your breath, then, is not just a simple biological function. Instead, it's a continuous reminder of your dependence on God. Each inhale gifts you with His sustenance; each exhale reminds you to trust in Him. It should not surprise you that in moments of anxiety when chaos threatens to overwhelm your inner world, returning to conscious awareness of breath can restore your connection with God. Breath heals.

However, as a follower of Christ, you must approach breathwork with both wisdom and discernment. The same breath that God gives for life and healing has been co-opted by various New Age practices that use regulated breathing as a gateway to altered states of consciousness. These types of experiences are outside of God's law. They can lead to encounters with entities that Scripture warns against.

Practices like Holotropic breathwork, while effective at helping with anxiety and trauma, can deliberately aim to separate consciousness from normal awareness. It can create experiences where you might feel you leave your body or encounter spiritual guides. As a Christian, you recognize that not all spiritual experiences are beneficial, regardless of how they might temporarily alleviate your symptoms.

The apostle Paul warns you to *"test the spirits to see whether they are from God"* (1 John 4:1). This testing applies not just to prophecy but to all spiritual practices, including how you engage with your breath. Your aim is never to seek wisdom from sources outside of God's revelation, but to be *"filled with the Spirit"* (Ephesians 5:18) as you present your body as a living sacrifice to God (Romans 12:1).

The breathing practices presented in this section are distinctly Christian in their approach. Through these Christ-centered breathing techniques, you can experience the calming of your nervous system without compromising your spiritual integrity. You can receive the gift of breath as it was intended. When it's done right, it can be an excellent way to help heal your anxiety.

Christian-Aligned Breathing Patterns for Anxiety

Here are specific breathing patterns you can incorporate into your Christian practice that help reduce anxiety while remaining spiritually aligned with your faith:

Box Breathing

One helpful technique is box breathing, also called four-square breathing. It's easy to learn and use. Here's how it works: breathe in through your nose while counting to four, hold your breath for another four counts, exhale slowly for four counts, and then pause for four more counts before starting over. This simple rhythm gives your mind something to focus on besides stress and helps your body relax.

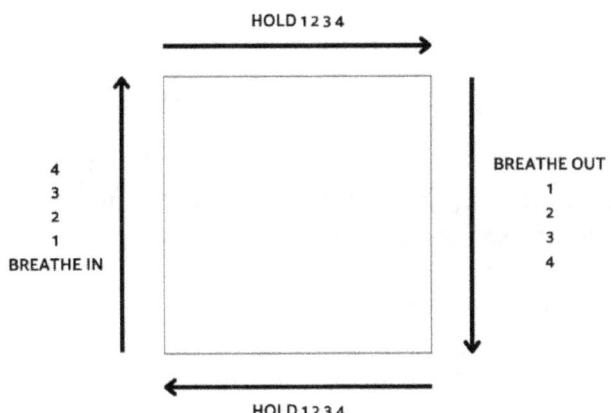

The 4-7-8 Scripture Breath

- Inhale through your nose for 4 counts (mentally recite: "I can do all things...")

- Hold for 7 counts (mentally complete: "...through Christ...")

- Exhale through your mouth for 8 counts (finish: "...who strengthens me." Philippians 4:13)
- Repeat 4 times

This breathing pattern activates the parasympathetic nervous system and combines physiological calming with scripture meditation.

The Psalm 46:10 Breath

- Inhale slowly for 5 counts
- Hold briefly (1 count)
- Exhale slowly for 5 counts while mentally saying "Be still and know that I am God"
- With each repetition, shorten the phrase:
  - "Be still and know that I am"
  - "Be still and know"
  - "Be still"
  - "Be"

This breathing pattern gradually brings your focus from anxious thoughts to simple presence with God.

The Armor of God Breathing Pattern

- Deep inhale while mentally saying "God has not given me a spirit of fear"
- Slow exhale while completing "but gives us power, love and self-discipline." (2 Timothy 1:7)
- Repeat 5-10 times while visualizing God's protection surrounding you

The Armor of God combines breath with spiritual protection imagery.

The Trinity Breath

- Inhale deeply through your nose for 3 counts (Father)
- Hold for 3 counts (Son)
- Exhale gently through your mouth for 3 counts (Holy Spirit)
- Repeat 7 times (representing completion)

This simple pattern is easy to remember during high anxiety moments

Breathwork Tips

- **Start Small**: Begin with just 3-5 minutes daily, perhaps as part of your morning prayer or devotional time
- **Use Physical Reminders**: Place scripture cards where you'll see them when anxiety strikes
- **Practice Regularly**: These techniques work better when practiced daily, not just during anxiety episodes
- **Frame Properly**: View these practices as physical stewardship of your body-temple and connection with God, not as spiritual techniques in themselves
- **Pair with Prayer**: Begin and end your breathing practice with simple prayer, acknowledging God's presence and requesting His peace

Remember that these breathing practices are tools to help you physically calm your body's stress response while maintaining focus on God. They're not meant to replace prayer, scripture reading, or Christian community, but to complement them as part of wholistic spiritual and physical self-care.

Using EFT to Clear Emotions

Emotional Freedom Techniques (EFT), which people commonly call tapping, is a therapeutic approach that unites traditional acupressure with contemporary psychological principles. The therapy requires light touch on body meridian points, including the forehead, collarbone, and hands, while concentrating on emotional issues or negative beliefs.

The process enables emotional blockages to release while stress reduces and the mind receives new positive beliefs.

To learn more about EFT, you can explore resources from experts like Gary Craig, the founder of EFT, or practitioners like Dawson Church and Nick Ortner.

There are websites such as The Tapping Solution (thetappingsolution.com) and EFT Universe (eftuniverse.com) that offer free guides, courses, and video demonstrations to help you get started. Brad Yates from Tap with Brad on YouTube (@tapwithbrad) has an extensive range of videos on tapping for different subjects. Best of all, it's free.

Using EMDR to Process Trauma

EMDR (Eye Movement Desensitization and Reprocessing) stands as a therapeutic method that guides patients through healing their distressing memories and trauma alongside anxiety and depression.

The therapy requires patients to concentrate on distressing memories under therapist-guided eye movement and audio or touch stimulation. The brain rewiring process through this method lowers emotional intensity in memories while establishing more beneficial cognitive pathways.

EMDR therapy helps patients overcome their emotional distress by treating its underlying causes instead of treating symptoms alone. Through its mechanism, the brain learns to restructure previous experiences until clients achieve both resolution and relief, which enhances their emotional stability and resilience.

To learn more about EMDR, you can visit the EMDR International Association (emdria.org) or The EMDR Institute (emdr.com), which provide research, training information, and directories to find certified therapists.

Understand that you will have many subconscious beliefs that need to be brought to the surface and worked through. It's not a one-off process, but an ongoing one. A single belief could take hours, days, or even weeks to clear.

Visualization to Clear Low Level Anxiety

For lower levels of anxiety, visualization exercises can help release the emotional charge stored in the body. Imagine the belief dissolving or visualize yourself handing it over to God, trusting that healing is happening. The process of belief transformation requires affirmations alongside self-compassion practice. Clearing emotions requires direct confrontation of emotions through awareness and questioning their validity before selecting a more loving perspective. These small actions will allow your new belief system to become permanent.

Healing Past Traumas with God's Help

When I was dealing with anxiety, bringing God into my healing process allowed me to change how I moved through the emotional pain I was feeling. This chapter focuses on a simple starting point: talking to God about your struggles and inviting Him into the places that hurt. Sharing your pain with Him builds trust and opens your heart to His comfort and grace. It's in these raw moments of honesty that healing can begin.

The Bible is full of stories that show God's ability to bring something beautiful out of brokenness. I personally loved the story of Joseph. I was inspired by how he went from being betrayed and enslaved to saving countless lives. David's story of finding restoration after his mistakes was helpful in my healing, too. When you're in the thick of things, reflecting on these examples can give you hope, reminding you that your pain isn't in vain and that God is still at work.

Prayer plays a big role in this process, especially when it comes to asking the Holy Spirit to help heal your old or traumatic wounds. It's not always easy to revisit painful memories, but doing so with God's presence can make it feel less overwhelming. Through specific prayers, you can ask Him to shine His light on those challenging places and help you see them through His love and compassion. It's important to take your time with this. Healing works on its own timeline. It was a tough lesson for me to remember that God works in His timing.

Forgiveness is another key part of letting go of what weighs you down. But let's be honest, it's not easy. Forgiveness doesn't mean saying what happened was okay or pretending it didn't hurt. Forgiveness means releasing the hold bitterness has on you so you can find peace. And you don't have to do it on your own. With God's strength, you can take those steps toward forgiving others and handing your pain over to Him. Here are some steps you can take to help with the forgiveness process:

- **Acknowledge your pain and emotions:** Make space to acknowledge the pain and anger along with the resentment you experience. Identify each emotion you feel and present these to God through prayer so He can comfort you and provide direction. Before you can forgive someone you need to openly discuss with Him what they did to hurt you.

- **Pray for strength and guidance:** Even when it feels impossible, ask God to help you forgive. Pray for the ability to see your situation through His eyes. If it feels too heavy, remember James' words: *"If any of you lacks wisdom, you should ask God, who gives generously to all without finding fault, and it will be given to you."* (James 1:5).

- **Reflect on God's forgiveness:** Consider how God has forgiven you through Christ. Meditating on scriptures like Ephesians 4:32, *"Be kind and compassionate to one another, forgiving each other, just as God forgave you in Christ."* can inspire you to extend grace to others.

- **Choose to forgive:** Forgiveness is a decision you need to make. It doesn't mean condoning what happened but releasing the hold it has on your heart. Tell God in prayer that you are choosing to forgive, even if the feelings of forgiveness take time to follow.

- **Let go of the desire for revenge:** Trust God to bring justice in His timing and way. Romans 12:19 reminds us, *"Do not take revenge... but leave room for God's wrath."* Letting go of the need to retaliate frees you from the burden of bitterness.

- **Seek reconciliation, if possible:** If it's safe and appropriate, reach out to the person who hurt you to share your feelings and seek understanding of the situation. While reconciliation may not always happen, forgiveness is for healing your own heart even without the other person's involvement. I personally haven't had much success with this. For me, it has proven to be better to work on forgiveness myself. Every situation and relationship is different, though.

- **Practice ongoing forgiveness:** Forgiveness isn't always a one-time act. Sometimes, you need to forgive repeatedly as new emotions surface. Keep turning to God for help as you continue to release the pain and choose peace.

- **Surround yourself with support:** Talk through the situation you need to forgive with people you trust. This could be a friend, a spiritual leader, or a professional counselor. They can give you support and perspective as you go through this emotional process.

If this feels overwhelming, structured prayers can be helpful. You might ask God to help you see the person who hurt you through His eyes or to give you the strength to let go of the anger you're holding onto. These prayers don't need to be perfect—just honest. Over time, they can help you tear down the walls that keep you from fully experiencing God's peace.

It's important to stay connected to God as you go through this process. Prayer isn't just about asking for help; it's a time when you can be totally honest with Him, no matter if you're feeling hopeful, angry, or a bit lost. Taking a little time each day to pray or reflect can really open up those important chats with God that help bring clarity and comfort.

Everyone experiences healing differently, and my own journey was significantly different from what I had anticipated. Christian faith plays a huge role, but it can also work hand in hand with other practices. Together, these tools can help you move forward with a sense of peace and hope for what's ahead.

Holding a Personal Healing Retreat with God

Imagine setting aside a weekend, free from the usual stress of daily life, to seek spiritual healing and direction. By dedicating this time to connect deeply with God, you create space for His peace to join with your spirit. For me, it was one of my favorite things I did to heal from anxiety. In fact, my own weekend with God contributed to a large part of my recovery. It led me to realize how deeply I needed to let go of trying to control everything and instead lean fully into His guidance.

That weekend became a turning point. It showed me not only how to reconnect with God but also how to use practical tools for healing. Through prayer, reflection, and learning about techniques like Holotropic breathwork, I began to understand how spiritual and physical practices could work together to help me heal. I'll share more about these discoveries, including the role of food, which became the most important aspect of my healing, in the future chapters.

When I first tried something like a personal retreat, I wasn't sure what to expect. I just knew I needed a break and some time alone with God. I started by setting aside two days where I wouldn't check my phone (I didn't even take it with me) or focus on my to-do list. Instead, I planned simple activities like prayer, fasting, journaling, and worship. It was like the ultimate dopamine detox with God by my side. And honestly? It felt like a deep breath for my soul.

You could start your retreat with prayer. I don't mean the kind where you tell Him a list of your worries, but a real conversation with God. Share what's been weighing you down and invite Him into those specific areas of your life. I've found that when I'm honest in my prayers—when I stop pretending I have it all together—it's easier to sense His peace and guidance.

Fasting was part of my dopamine detox. It was definitely a little intimidating! It's not about making yourself miserable. Instead, it helps you to shift your focus from physical things to spiritual ones. Maybe you skip a meal or decide not to eat until a certain time. When the cravings hit, use that moment to lean into God and ask Him to fill the deeper hunger in your heart.

Journaling can be surprisingly powerful during a retreat like this. I like to write out my prayers, the thoughts that won't leave my mind, and even random things I feel God might be saying to me. Sometimes I just can't wrap my head or heart around things until I put pen to paper. It really helps me to figure it all out. When I look back, I often see things more clearly in those raw and emotional pages. It also shows me where I'm feeling sorry for myself or trying to control my life.

Then there's music, which is such a sweet way to reconnect with God. Whether you sing along to your favorite worship songs or just sit quietly and let the music wash over you, it's a chance to let go of the stress you've been carrying. I've had moments where a song just unlocked something in me, and before I knew it, I was crying tears I didn't even know I needed to cry. I also use soft instrumental music to keep me calm while I read at night. It helps me block out the rest of the world. It is preferable to avoid technology during your retreat, so singing is the best in this circumstance. However, you know what you need and what will work best for you.

Throughout the weekend, you might also take some time to sit in silence. At first, it might be a bit challenging, particularly if you're accustomed to a lot of noise, but silence and/or meditation can help you calm your mind and simply be with God. In those quiet moments, you might find that you can hear Him most clearly, like a soft nudge or a warm presence.

During my retreat, I realized how much God desired to meet me in my current state, complete with anxieties and doubts. You don't have to be perfect or have everything figured out to spend time with Him. He's ready to bring peace to the parts of your heart that feel unsettled, one step at a time.

When your weekend ends, take a moment to look back at everything you experienced. What stood out to you? Was there a prayer, a verse, or even just a feeling of God's presence that felt significant? Write those things down so you can hold onto them.

And don't stop there. Build on what you started. Maybe you keep journaling or add a few minutes of silence to your daily routine. The retreat might be over, but the intimate connection you've created with God doesn't have to end. Little by little, you'll find new ways to bring what you experienced into your everyday life.

Identifying Spiritual Strongholds in Prayer

When it comes to anxiety, it's worth considering that some of what you're feeling might come from deeper spiritual struggles. It's not always easy to recognize, but there could be underlying spiritual strongholds—patterns of fear or beliefs that have taken root in your heart and keep feeding the anxiety. Inviting God into the process can make all the difference. When you ask Him to shine a light on those hidden areas, you open yourself up to healing in a way that goes far beyond what you might figure out on your own.

I've experienced this myself. There were times when I thought my anxiety was just about the stress of life, but when I brought it to God, He gently showed me fears I'd been holding onto for years—things I didn't even realize were affecting me. Those moments felt like God turning on a light in a dark room, helping me see clearly what needed His touch.

Come to God and ask Him to reveal anything subconscious fears or beliefs that are fueling your anxiety. It might feel scary at first—like opening a door to a room you've avoided for a long time—but remember that God is there for you with love and grace, not judgment.

This process isn't meant to be tackled alone. Sometimes, we need trusted people to help us recognize what we can't see on our own. A pastor, a mentor, or a dear Christian friend can provide valuable perspective and wisdom. I've had some lovely chats with my pastor, and he's helped me see patterns I hadn't noticed before. His prayers have really lifted me up and encouraged me to keep moving ahead.

Another important step is asking God to help you recognize lies the enemy might be planting in your mind. Anxiety can sometimes feel like a constant loop of worst-case scenarios and self-doubt. The enemy loves to twist the truth and keep you stuck in that cycle. Through prayer, you can learn to identify those lies and replace them with God's word.

The more you take these spiritual strongholds to God and lean on your community to support you, the better things will start to get. As your anxiety begins to lighten, you make space for peace and a stronger sense of freedom. And here's the thing: it's not just about managing your anxiety. These are deeper issues that can change your relationship with God. There is a resulting joy that occurs when you give your worries over to Him, even in the middle of life's difficulties.

If you're not sure where to begin, spend a few minutes praying about the spiritual roots of your anxiety. Don't rush through it and ask God for clarity. Close your eyes and let it sit. Sometimes the breakthroughs happen while just sitting quietly and listening. You can also record patterns and themes to track over time.

Concluding Thoughts

In this chapter, we've looked at practical ways to deal with anxiety in your daily life. Taking the time to identify your triggers and write them down helps you see what's really happening and how to move forward. The way I dealt with this was by setting small, manageable goals each week. You should check in with yourself to reflect, adjust, or celebrate your progress, no matter how small. Carving out a few moments for relaxation, whether it's deep breaths or quiet prayer, is something to fall back on when life is unpredictable.

Anxiety management isn't one size fits all, but when you pair practical strategies with your faith, you're building yourself a foundation that speaks to both your emotional and spiritual needs. This is all about figuring out what is going to work for your special situation and believing God will meet you in the process and give you fresh hope and newfound strength to continue on.

There's more to come, but if you are enjoying this book so far, I'd be so grateful if you could take a moment to leave an honest review on Amazon. Your thoughts help other readers decide if this book is right for them and support independent authors like me. Reviews don't have to be long—even a few sentences sharing your experience with the book make a big difference!

If you have any feedback or concerns, I'd love to hear from you directly. Feel free to reach out to me at grace@wingsofgracepublishing.com

I truly appreciate your support and the time you've taken to read this book! If you feel called to, please leave a review so other anxious Christians can find the help they need. Your words of love also help me as an author to inspire as many people as I can. You can leave your review here: http://links.wingsofgracepublishing.com/anxiety-book or use the QR code below.

Chapter 6: Sustaining Long-Term Peace

A lot of Christians struggle to find lasting peace, especially when the curveballs just don't stop coming. Those quiet, reflective moments (which are helpful) are not the only thing that can help you heal. It's your everyday choices that add up to create a sense of calm and serenity.

Creating long-term peace needs your time and focus. The best way is to build up the kind of habits that will help you stay grounded and happy. The right habits and ability to sustain calmness will help you feel steadier when things get a little chaotic. God placed you here to thrive in His name, not just to survive. You need to make room in your heart for God's light, and that means reducing your anxiety so you can enjoy your relationship with Him.

Building Habits for Lasting Change

If you're like me, some days can feel like a whirlwind, and finding moments of tranquility is a challenge. Create a rhythm that helps you stay calm, even when things around you seem chaotic. If you're looking to build a habit that brings you peace, it's more valuable than just ticking items off a list. As I found out for myself, having a structured day can really make a difference. I didn't want to add extra tasks to my already over-scheduled calendar, but I was interested in setting up habits that reduced my stress and gave me space to breathe.

How about we kick things off with something easy? Like making your bed every morning. It might seem like a small thing, but it's a nice way to begin your day and bring some order to the craziness. It might seem trivial, but it really changes how you cope with the rest of your day. When you stop to think about it, making your bed is a joyful little win. It helps you take control of your emotions instead of letting them take charge of you.

Now you've got your bed making out of the way, it's time to set some healthy boundaries. When you're healing from anxiety, you may need to say no to things or people that drain you. The best place to start is to remove as many tasks from your busy days as possible. What can you outsource or get help for? What can you reduce? Can you go part-time at work? How can you save time so you have time to heal? I've learned that it's okay to put mental health first and create the space needed for peace.

Here's a list of tasks you could outsource or simplify without breaking the bank:

1. **Grocery Shopping:** Use online services or pickup options. If you have a consistent range of food that you purchase frequently, this is even faster.

2. **Meal Prep at Home:** Set aside a couple of hours to prepare your meals for the week ahead or arrange for a batch cooking session with friends. You can also swap some meals, which will provide you with a variety of dishes to try.

3. **Meal Prep Made Easy:** Buy pre-chopped vegetables and foods, or buy ready-made meals or use meal kits for easy cooking.

4. **Cleaning:** Hire a cleaner for a few hours a month or use an app to find local, affordable help.

5. **Laundry:** Use a local laundromat's wash-and-fold service or find someone locally to help you.

6. **Errands:** Delegate tasks like dry cleaning or package returns through apps or local services.

7. **Yard Work:** Hire neighborhood teens or small local businesses for mowing or weeding.

8. **Dog Walking:** Use affordable apps or ask a neighbor or friend for help.

9. **Pet Care:** Find low-cost pet sitters or daycares for when you're busy.

10. **Childcare:** Swap babysitting duties with friends or neighbors for free or give a local teenager some paid work experience.

11. **Tutoring:** Use online platforms or local college students for inexpensive help with kids' homework.

12. **Administrative Tasks:** Use a virtual assistant for scheduling, managing emails, or organizing files.

13. **Social Media Management:** If you run a small business, hire affordable freelancers for online tasks.

14. **Digital File Cleanup:** Hire a virtual assistant to organize your computer files or emails.

15. **DIY Repairs:** Hire a handyman for repairs instead of tackling stressful projects yourself.

16. **Organizing:** Find a local organizer to tidy up your space or sort through clutter.

17. **Subscription Management:** Use apps to track and cancel unused subscriptions for you or comb through your bank statements to find them.

One of the things that really helps me is setting aside time for prayer or scripture reading. Every morning, I take a few quiet moments where I can just sit with God. In fact, this has become my non-negotiable, even if my bed doesn't get made! 99% of the time, I manage to make my bed, and I use the next few moments to spend time with God.

Sometimes, I use the morning time to memorize a Bible verse. If I'm struggling with anxiety, I'll use a verse I like, *"Peace I leave with you; my peace I give you. I do not give to you as the world gives. Do not let your hearts be troubled and do not be afraid."* (John 14:27) I say it over and over, letting it sink in. When I remember these truths, they remind me that I am supported, and I can trust God to handle the day ahead.

Affirmations can also be a powerful tool. I maintain a list of faith-based affirmations, such as "God's peace guards my heart and mind today," which I repeat every morning. Just saying affirmations out loud helps shift my mindset and center me in God's promises. It's amazing how something as simple as speaking these truths can calm my mind and fill me with peace.

Here are a few affirmations you can try:

- I am wonderfully made by God.
- God's peace guards my heart and mind today.
- I trust in God's plan for my life, even when I can't see it all clearly.
- I am never alone. God is with me every step of the way.
- With God, I am stronger than my fears.
- I am more than a conqueror through Christ, who loves me.
- God's love casts out all my fears.
- I am worthy of peace and joy, for I am God's child.
- God provides me with everything I need for today.
- I choose to trust God's timing and rest in His provision.
- God's grace is sufficient for me in every situation.
- I am capable and empowered because God is with me.
- I release my anxieties to God, knowing He cares for me.
- I am a vessel of God's peace and love to the world around me.
- Each new day is a gift from God, full of His mercy and grace.
- My hope is in the Lord, and my foundation is faith.
- Through Christ, I can do all things and overcome every challenge.
- I am surrounded by God's favor and protection today.
- God is my refuge and strength. He is present to help me in times of trouble.

Try saying them aloud in the morning or whenever you feel the need to realign your thoughts. Place a few different ones around your home. It's a simple way to remind yourself that God's got you covered, no matter what's going on around you.

Taking time for self-care is just as important. I don't mean a fancy spa day, though they are wonderful. Self-care can be as simple as taking a walk or taking a moment to sit and reflect. Even spending time doing something you love—whether it's reading the Bible or gardening—can help you recharge. For me, I need to make those moments a priority. If I don't, I can easily burn out.

Sometimes, the stress in life comes from not knowing how to respond to everything that's thrown our way. That's where mindfulness really helps. When faced with something challenging, slow down, breathe deeply, and decide how you want to handle it. I've learned that when I take a few seconds to pause and breathe, I'm better equipped to deal with whatever comes my way. For me, it's been life-changing to practice being present in the moment, especially when anxiety tries to take over.

Then there's Sabbath rest, which I think is an important day for modern Christians. I know it can be difficult to take a break, but committing to a slow and relaxing day—whether it's Sundays or another day that fits into your week—gives you permission to slow down. I make it a day to focus on God and connect with loved ones. I also avoid any stressful tasks. I can tell you that doing this has really helped me reset. Pushing harder isn't the answer. The real focus is on trusting God and allowing yourself time to recharge.

Another practice that helped me was designing a space in my home specifically for peace. I briefly mentioned this earlier, but I created a little corner in my bedroom where I can go to pray or reflect. It's filled with things that remind me of God's love—a Bible verse on the wall and a candle I light when I pray, along with a few trinkets and a cross. Having a dedicated space helps me slow down, focus, and connect with God.

All these little habits, when done consistently, add up. You don't have to do everything all at once. Try some and see what works for you. Celebrate the little victories along the way, like making it through a tough day or simply being able to pause and pray in the middle of a busy moment. Each step is part of a bigger picture—creating a life that's rooted in peace, grounded in faith, and full of moments where you can experience God's presence.

Remember, it's moving forward that matters most, not reaching some idealized version of perfection. In fact, let go of the need for perfection in any part of your life. Everything you can do to move yourself toward increased peace and calmness counts.

Speaking of calm, do everything you can to create a peaceful life. Distance yourself from as much negativity as possible, including the daily news on TV (there's nothing positive about that!), other people's dramas, and anything else that causes you anxiety. Believe it or not, I haven't watched the news in over 20 years, yet I haven't missed much. If something is important that affects my world, someone will tell me about it.

Trust that with God's help, you can create a routine that supports your mental health and helps you grow in faith. Keep leaning into His strength, and know that even in the busy moments, you're not alone.

Learning to Have a Peaceful Mindset

Making small, thoughtful changes to your daily routine is the first step toward finding peace when you're feeling anxious. Being thankful is a fantastic place to begin. When you pause to thank God for even the little things—a friend's kind word, the beauty of a sunrise, or a magical moment in your day—you start to notice the world in a whole new way. It's kind of like wearing glasses that let you see God's goodness right in front of your eyes. I've found that when I start my day by writing down three things I'm thankful for, it softens my heart and sets a peaceful tone, no matter what the day brings.

Relationships also play a huge role in how peaceful your life is. Surrounding yourself with positive people who truly care about you makes a difference. These are the friends and relatives who will pray with you, encourage you, and remind you of God's way when you forget. I've been blessed with a few close friends who are my spiritual lifelines. They've walked with me through challenging times, and their prayers and support have helped me find peace when I couldn't on my own.

With the ability to have our phone in hand every waking minute, it's so easy to get lost in scrolling and clicking. Before you know it, you're hopping from one notification to another. But all that chaos will cause you to feel a bit on edge. Putting some limits on technology, especially social media, can change things up. How about taking a few small breaks from your phone or computer during the day? I've begun dedicating an hour each evening to leaving my phone in another room and just letting my mind relax. Depending on the night, I may spend that time reading scripture, chatting with God, or simply relaxing in the quiet. It's amazing how stepping away from screens can really let God's peace wash over your heart.

I also frequently do a 24-hour dopamine detox. As I previously mentioned, I do this when I'm on a retreat with God. The goal is to reduce everything that causes over-stimulation, including TV, the internet, junk food, sugar, and interactions with people; some people even go so far as not speaking to anyone! It's up to you how seriously you want to take it if you do choose to complete a dopamine detox.

One excellent way to bring some calm into your day is to use prayer cards whenever anxiety starts to sneak in. Write down a verse like Colossians 3:15: *"Let the peace of Christ rule in your hearts, since as members of one body, you were called to peace. And be thankful,"* or a short prayer asking for God's calm. Keep them in places where you'll see them often. It could be on your desk, in your car, or taped to your bathroom mirror. I've found it comforting to have those little reminders when my mind starts racing. They're like tiny whispers from God, nudging you back to peace whenever you feel overwhelmed.

When everything feels like too much, focusing on one thing at a time can help ease the weight. Take a breath and ask God for clarity. Instead of staring down a never-ending to-do list, choose one task and give it your full attention. Reduce overwhelm by having a maximum of three must-do tasks per day.

I've learned that when I rush through tasks or try to juggle too much, I end up more anxious and frustrated. But when I pause, pray, and tackle one thing with a calm, steady focus, I feel more at peace. Let God guide your steps, trusting Him to help you manage the rest in His timing.

Incorporating Self-Care Practices

Caring for your mind and body doesn't mean you're being extravagant; it's part of honoring the life God has given you. Sometimes, as Christians, we confuse selflessness with neglecting our own needs. But let me tell you from my own experience, it's not. When I tried to ignore my own needs, I found myself drained, snippy, and far less able to be present for the people I care about. Taking time to recharge isn't just good for you; it's a way to honor the body and mind God has entrusted to you.

Stress is an inescapable aspect of life, yet the way you manage it can significantly impact your outcomes. Maybe right in this moment you aren't handling stress all that well. That's okay. Acknowledging it is the first step toward change. With a few small, intentional shifts, you can start finding healthier ways to respond and invite peace back into your life.

Have you ever actually paused in the middle of a hectic day to just breathe? Do you do that regularly? Those pauses have saved me countless times from ending up a wreck on the bathroom floor at work. A walk during your lunch break for a few minutes, reading some scripture between tasks, or a quick prayer of gratitude can change your day more than you imagine. I like to think of them as mini resets; little reminders that God's peace is always available, even in the chaos.

And here's something I've learned the hard way: you've got to make space for the things that bring you joy. Maybe it's painting, playing a musical instrument, baking, or tending to a garden. For me, it's writing. It's my outlet, my way to process and connect with God's creativity. These moments of joy refill your cup and remind you that life isn't just a to-do list; it's also meant to be enjoyed.

Self-care also has a spiritual side. Taking care of yourself helps you show up better for others. When you're well rested and grounded, aren't you more patient, more loving? When you put your well-being first, you are better positioned to serve the people in your family, friends, or church community. That's stewardship: making the most of the life God has given you so that you might carry out His will.

Adding small, meaningful habits into your day can lay the groundwork for long-term peace. I'm not referring to the common advice, such as drinking enough water, getting sufficient sleep, or beginning your morning with prayer or gratitude. For me, mornings are key. I make my coffee, sit in my favorite chair, and take a few minutes to think about how good God is. It's not fancy, but it helps me start the day with a clearer head and a calmer heart.

In the end, self-care isn't about being indulgent; it's about being intentional with our lives. When we incorporate these practices into our daily routine, we can really enjoy a life filled with health, happiness, and sustainability. Self-care is an important part of mental well-being, and embracing it helps create a life of peace and purpose. When we commit to self-care, we are fulfilling a divine responsibility to ourselves—to act in accordance with our values and our faith. Through this alignment, we can live authentically and compassionately, ready to accept the blessings of each new day. Self-care not only makes us better people, but it also makes us better partners and better members of our communities, and that ripples out to all parts of our lives.

Handling Relapses of Anxiety with Grace

When you've been working so hard to find peace, relapses can be discouraging. When moments of anxiety or overwhelm strike, it's easy to believe that you're back at the beginning, but that's not the case at all. Setbacks are part of healing, and they don't define your progress. The reality is, as Christians, we know God's grace meets us in every moment, even in the messy or challenging ones. In this section, we'll look at how to manage relapses with compassion, faith, and practical strategies that can guide you through these worrying times.

Acknowledge That Relapses Happen

Unfortunately, relapses are just a part of life. They happen to all of us. This doesn't mean you're failing or not making progress. Anxiety sometimes comes back with full force, and there's nothing you can do about it. It doesn't mean you haven't come a long way already. When things aren't going as planned, you can feel discouraged. You need to understand that your setbacks do not define you. Grace meets even when you feel like you're far from peace. When anxiety does strike again, you'll have a plan on how to handle it. Even the strongest Christians face struggles. It's part of being human. Just look at the Bible. Some of the most faithful people went through tough times, doubting, worrying, and struggling, but God never left them. Just remember that when anxiety returns, you're not starting from scratch. You have come a long way, and God is still right there. Relapses aren't the end of the world; they're just a bump in the road. You can always return to God's love and peace when you need it.

Refuse to Let Guilt Take Root

It's common to feel guilt sneak in when anxiety returns. You may find yourself wondering, 'Shouldn't I be past this by now?' or 'What's holding me back from getting it together?' I truly get it. It feels like you're on the right track, but then your anxiety just pops up out of nowhere. It can be overwhelming, particularly when you've made significant progress in your mental health. But here's the truth: guilt is a trap, and it doesn't help anyone, especially you.

When anxiety flares up, the enemy loves to use guilt as a weapon. He wants you to feel like you've failed, like you're somehow falling short of God's expectations. But that's a lie. God doesn't keep track of your mistakes like that. His grace is bigger than any setback you are having. Hebrews 10:22—*"Let us draw near to God with a sincere heart and with the full assurance that faith brings, having our hearts sprinkled to cleanse us from a guilty conscience and having our bodies washed with pure water."* That means when anxiety comes back, you don't need to beat yourself up over it. God's mercy still covers you, and you continue to walk in His grace.

It helps to remind yourself that being human means facing struggles. Even the Apostle Paul talked about feeling weak and burdened. He wasn't always in control. No one is. So, when you're feeling overwhelmed or defeated, try to shift your focus from guilt to God's love. Remind yourself that you are exactly where you need to be. Healing isn't linear, and neither is growth. Some days will be better than others.

Instead of giving space to guilt, let God's love and mercy take the lead. Talk to Him about how you're feeling—whether it's frustration, doubt, or sadness. He can handle it. And instead of sitting in guilt, look at this moment as a chance to lean into His grace even more. His love isn't dependent on your ability to always get it right. It's unconditional. And that love will carry you through even the toughest of days. Guilt can't grow where grace is abundant, so choose to hold onto the truth that you're loved and protected by God.

Practice Compassion Toward Yourself

Can you remember when a friend of yours was going through a rough patch? Perhaps they were facing some anxiety, or maybe they just had a few negative hits in a row. What did you do? Did you criticize them for their struggles? Did you tell them to "snap out of it" or "get over it?" It's unlikely. Instead, you probably sat down with a warm cup of tea or coffee and shared some of your kind words with them. You no doubt listened and empathized and probably gave them a hug. You reminded them that God is with them, and tough days are okay. Why should you treat yourself differently?

When you're facing setbacks, whether it's a relapse of anxiety or just an overwhelming day, you have to show yourself the same compassion. We tend to be our own harshest critics, don't we? When things aren't going well, we can be quick to point out our flaws and feel like we're falling short. I know I've had my share of moments where I've thought, "Why can't I handle this better? Why am I still struggling with this?" But guess what? We don't hold other people to the same impossible standards we set for ourselves. If your friend came to you feeling defeated, you wouldn't lecture them. You'd give them the grace they need to move forward. You deserve that same grace.

Setbacks are not signs of failure. Really, they're just moments to stop, breathe, and lean into God. He's never holding your mistakes against you, so why should you? Every time you slip or feel overwhelmed, remember that this is just part of being human. You don't have to be perfect. If anything, these moments are invitations to start fresh and turn to God for strength, not to beat yourself up.

When I've had days where I feel like I've fallen short, I remind myself that it's okay to step back, give myself some grace, and try again tomorrow. Sometimes that looks like sitting in a quiet space and letting the weight of my emotions rest before I get back into trying to "fix" things. God isn't looking for perfection; He's looking for your heart. Showing compassion to yourself isn't a sign of weakness; it's an act of faith. You're trusting that God's grace is enough for you in this moment and that He's already got it covered.

So next time you face a setback, pause and take a deep breath. Give yourself some space to just be. You don't have to have it all together. You're doing the best you can, and that's enough. Just like you would with a friend, remind yourself that you are loved, you are enough, and it's okay to take a break and lean into God's grace. He's not in a rush, so there's no need for you to be either.

Pray Honestly and Without Shame

Praying honestly is one of the most freeing things you can do, especially when anxiety strikes. It's so easy to feel like you should hide your struggles, thinking God won't understand or that you should be "stronger" by now. But God already knows what's on your heart. When you're feeling overwhelmed, He wants to hear your raw, unfiltered thoughts. You don't have to have the perfect words. In fact, sometimes just telling God, "I'm scared" or "I don't know what to do" is enough. I've found that when I open up to God like this, I feel a wave of peace rolling over me that's difficult to explain. It's like a sense of being held and understood. There's no shame in bringing your struggles to Him. He's not disappointed in you. He's right there, offering comfort and reminding you that you're never facing this alone.

Create a Relapse Response Plan

When anxiety flares up, having a relapse reaction plan can be a huge help. It doesn't need to be complicated, just a few simple steps to follow when you're feeling overwhelmed.

For me, having scriptures like Matthew 6:34 ready to go has been a comfort. *"Therefore, do not worry about tomorrow, for tomorrow will worry about itself. Each day has enough trouble of its own."*

I'm always reminding myself that Jesus invites me to bring my burdens to Him, and He promises rest for my soul. It's tough to think straight when anxiety hits. It really helps to have a list of calming activities ready to go. I've learned to just go outside for a 10-minute walk, sit in silence for a little bit, or even take a quick coffee break, and it has really helped me feel so much better. It's amazing what a little pause can do! The key is knowing what works for you and having a list of these simple actions ready to go. It's like having a toolbox of peace, and just knowing you have a plan can break the cycle of anxiety.

Revisit What Worked Before

When anxiety shows up again, you may feel like you've gone back to square one and have become stuck in the same loop. Remember those times when peace finally cut through all the chaos? What did you use to comfort yourself then? Perhaps it was something small. Those moments aren't accidents; they're little signposts pointing you back to His faithfulness. When I'm feeling overwhelmed, I like to think back to how God was there for me during a similar time. It's a subtle message from God: 'We've been here before, and I'll take you through again.' Don't be scared to go back to those moments. They remind you that God's love for you is constant, even when you might not feel that way.

Keep a "God's Faithfulness" Journal

Sometimes, in the middle of a challenging bout of anxiety, everything feels overwhelming. It's easy to forget the ways God has been there for you before. That's why keeping a journal of God's faithfulness can help you move past whatever is difficult during a relapse. Write down the times when He answered a prayer, sent just the right person into your life to help, or gave you strength when you didn't think you could keep going. These notes can be short and simple—just tiny reminders of His goodness in your life. When anxiety creeps in, re-reading your journal can feel like having a conversation with your past self. It will give you faith that God showed up then, and He'll show up now. I've found this practice not only builds my faith but helps me shift my focus from fear to faith, even when it's hard.

Write a Letter to Your Future Self

There's something powerful about hearing encouragement in your own words. In your 'God's Faithfulness' journal, take the time to write a letter to the future you. Imagine reading it when you're going through a rough patch and anxiety is pulling you down. What would you want to hear? Remind yourself of God's unshakable love and how He's been there for you before. Speak truth over your future struggles, pointing yourself back to His promises. You might even include a few kind words, the kind you'd share with a dear friend who's going through a difficult time. I've done this, and it's almost like getting a pep talk from someone who knows exactly what you need to hear. That's because it came from you. When things feel overwhelming, that letter can be a lifeline, grounding you in truth and offering a glimpse of hope on the other side.

Pray for Others Who Are Struggling

Another way to find some relief from anxiety is by praying for others who might be feeling just as anxious as you. It's a simple activity that helps you look beyond yourself, reminding you that there are others out there who could really use a hand. When I pray for others, I find that it helps me to see things differently. It makes me think of how God is working in their lives just as He is in mine. It could be someone in your church, a friend, or even a stranger you've heard of who's going through a rough patch. Supporting them from a distance is as easy as lifting them up in prayer. As you ask God to bring them peace, you might just begin to feel His peace settling into your own heart as well.

Do One Small Act of Service

Shifting your focus toward helping someone else isn't the first thing that comes to mind when you're anxious. I've found that even the smallest acts of service can bring a sense of perspective and connection. One day while I was out shopping, I was finding it difficult to concentrate on anything other than my own anxious thoughts. While I was leaving a store, I spotted an elderly man making his way to the entrance. He was trying to balance his shopping bags and his cane. I moved aside and opened the door for him. He stopped, looked up at me, and smiled at me. He quietly replied, "Thank you, dear." That seemingly simple and almost unplanned moment of connection felt like a little bit of kindness, reminding me that even when my mind is racing, there is room for connection.I thought back to the fact that God created us to be in community with one another—lifting one another up without even knowing it. You might not feel like you're doing much, but there's a ripple effect. They remind you that you're part of something bigger—a shared kindness and love that reflects God's love in the everyday.

Relapses are not roadblocks; they're reminders that you are human. God and Jesus deeply love you, and you are on the path toward peace. When you lean into God's faithfulness, being honest with yourself, and showing yourself the same grace He offers, you can handle those moments with strength and confidence. Just do what you can with the tools you've got. Keep moving ahead, even if the steps you're taking are tiny. God is right there with you through every struggle, offering you strength, comfort, and a never-ending supply of grace.

A Final Word on Peace

Sustaining long-term peace is something we often wish for, but it's not always easy. Life can present unexpected challenges, and anxiety can creep in without warning. But peace isn't something we just find once and then forget about. It's something we create daily.

You might have days when peace feels out of reach. I know I've had those moments, too. But what I've learned is that peace doesn't depend on everything being perfect. It's all about coming back to God's love each day, no matter how often we trip up.

Even when things get a bit chaotic, you can always find a little peace if you look for it. God's peace isn't contingent on our circumstances but based in His presence. The more we get into the habit of turning to Him, the more we get to experience His peace, whatever comes.

Don't get discouraged by setbacks or let them get the better of you. Just keep showing up and trusting the process. God's peace isn't contingent on our circumstances but based in His presence. Turning to Him more often helps us experience His peace no matter what we're dealing with.

"When you make a mistake, respond to yourself in a loving way rather than a self-shaming way."

~ Ellie Holcomb ~

Chapter 7: Connecting with the Christian Community

We've touched on this briefly before, but let's go a bit deeper. Getting involved with a Christian community can help you find emotional support and a sense of belonging. While your relationship with God is deeply personal, He never intended for you to walk this path alone. A lot of churches offer support networks that can help you through life's ups and downs. If you're dealing with anxiety, fear, worry, or depression, your local church community could be an excellent resource for support. Here's what I want you to know: your church family can be a beautiful source of comfort. Often, there is one person who greets you with a warm hug or engages in a friendly chat that instantly puts you at ease. I've experienced it myself. There's something unique about being with other Christians who understand.

Finding Supportive Groups within Your Church

Your local church congregation can be a powerful way to receive emotional support. It gives you access to different people from unique backgrounds, many of whom would be happy to be connected with you and help out. Larger congregations tend to have different support groups available. But even if your church doesn't, there's no reason you couldn't start one yourself.

Because people experience anxiety in different ways, starting a small group could help you and others find the help you need. Everyone handles anxiety in different ways, and someone in your group might have overcome an issue you're facing. Members of these groups often feel less afraid to talk about their experiences because they can share their fears and anxieties with other like-minded people. The right group dynamic can offer empathy and understanding. By sharing your challenges with others, you'll learn the steps other members have taken to overcome theirs. And while their situations may not be the same as yours, often the modes of healing cross over to different issues.

Then there's the incredible value of being mentored in your community. Perhaps your mentor is someone who has experienced similar struggles and can provide genuine, useful guidance—someone who truly understands. Mentorship can significantly transform your life, particularly if you're uncertain about conventional guidance but still desire to express your faith in a genuine and grounded manner. A mentor can offer wisdom that not only gives you peace in your current struggles but also strengthens your relationship with God, helping you see how faith and emotional well-being can go hand in hand.

It's common to feel nervous about taking the first step toward engaging with a community, but honestly, once you do, it's worth it. There's something so special about being part of a group where people care about your emotions and your growth. Whether you're there for an event, a group session, or even just a quick chat with a new friend, these connections build up over time. They help nurture both your emotional healing and your spiritual growth. Each new relationship you form brings you closer to finding peace—whether it's peace in your mind or peace in your heart, it all matters.

Taking that first step to engage can feel like a leap, but once you do, you'll see that the community around you becomes a place of support and love that makes the challenging days easier and the positive days even better.

Participating in Church Events

Let me share with you how getting involved in church activities has helped me. It might help you on your path to freedom from anxiety.

There's something about walking into church on Sunday morning. The familiar faces, the friendly greetings, and the soft worship music all combine to create a wonderful sense of coming home. I used to think I needed to "get myself together" before showing up to church. But you know what? I reminded myself that God accepts us as we are, including anxious thoughts, racing hearts, and all.

Remember what Jesus said in Matthew 11:28? *"Come to me, all you who are weary and burdened, and I will give you rest."* It's a promise, and I've seen it come true week after week.

My close friend, Sarah, has struggled with panic attacks for years. She felt overwhelmed in crowds and avoided a lot of public places. In fact, she was bordering on agoraphobia. But she made a commitment to come to church every Sunday, even if she had to sit in the back row near the door. Over time, she found herself moving closer to the front, one row at a time. She found that the faces that were familiar soon became friends, and worship time became her weekly reset button.

If you go regularly, you start to notice little things. Perhaps you find yourself relaxing in the familiarity of worship, or you look forward to seeing someone. These small moments add up to a reminder that there are people around you who care.

Retreats and Conferences

I will never forget the first Christian retreat I attended after receiving an anxiety diagnosis. I was scared to be out of my comfort zone, but those three days were the exact thing my soul needed. Stepping away from your normal routine and spending some focused time with God and fellow Christians is powerful.

At retreats, you often find yourself sharing meals with people who understand exactly what you're going through. I remember sitting around a campfire with five other women, sharing our stories of anxiety and faith. A woman shared with us how she used to keep her panic attacks a secret from everyone at church. I used to do the same. Just like I had, though, she learned that being vulnerable could actually be a gift to those around her. We found ourselves praying together, shedding some tears, and sharing a good laugh. It was truly healing.

Conferences can also be wonderful, although they differ from retreats in some ways. Retreats are more intimate; conferences are more high-energy and motivating. I've learned practical strategies during conferences for dealing with anxious thoughts without losing my footing in Scripture and met some amazing people who have become prayer partners and friends. The great thing is Christian conferences include a focus on modern-day struggles, and that is something so many of us need.

Involvement in Community Service

Here's something that might surprise you. Some of my most peaceful moments have come while serving others through church programs. It's amazing how much can heal when you put your energy into helping someone else. Sometimes, your own worries end up being pushed aside.

Last year, I volunteered at my church's food pantry when they were short staffed. Honestly, I was nervous at first. I kept thinking, 'What if I mess something up? What if I don't know what to say to people?' But those fears didn't stick around for long. As soon as I started packing boxes with groceries and talking to the other volunteers, I felt a sense of peace I hadn't expected.

Mary, who had been running the pantry for years, has this way of putting things into perspective. She always said, "We're not just feeding people's stomachs; we're showing them God's love." And you know what? She was absolutely right. Every interaction, whether I was handing over a bag of food or sharing a quick smile, feels like a small way of saying, 'You're seen. You're cared for.'

It's not just about helping others; it can touch your own heart, too. Those hours at the pantry were some of the most meaningful moments of my year. Working alongside others who share your faith creates bonds that go deeper than casual friendship. When we were serving together, we were living out our faith in a tangible way. As we focused on blessing others, God could use these moments to bring healing and peace to our own hearts.

Engagement in Workshops and Bible Studies

Can I tell you about something that really opened my eyes? It was during a small group Bible study on Philippians 4:6-7 (the verses about anxiety and prayer I've mentioned previously). We were discussing what it really means to "not be anxious about anything" when Linda, our group leader, shared her own struggles with anxiety. "For years," she said, "I thought this verse meant I was failing as a Christian because I still got anxious. Then I realized that it's not about never feeling anxiety; it's about what we do with it when it comes."

Bible studies are so valuable because of these kinds of honest discussion. You are not just learning about Scripture. You are seeing it applied to real life, real struggles, and real people just like you. In the small group setting, you'll have space to ask questions, share concerns, and learn from others who are a few steps ahead of you on this path.

Workshops can be incredibly helpful, too. In the workshop our church recently hosted, the speaker taught us practical ways to use Scripture during anxious moments, like writing verses on index cards to keep in our purses or cars. These are more than coping techniques. They are ways to strengthen our faith and trust in God's faithfulness.

I want to tell you something important. That doesn't mean your anxiety disqualifies you from being an active part of church life. In many ways, this might be what makes your participation so meaningful—as well as meaningful for others who are silently struggling.

When you're choosing to show up to Sunday service or a volunteer opportunity, you're stepping into your faith. Every time you tell your story in a Bible study or meet a person at a retreat, you're extending as well as receiving hope. Remember, the church isn't a showcase for perfect people. It is a family of Christians who are all growing, learning, and healing together. Your presence matters. Your story matters. Most importantly, your healing matters to God.

Key Takeaways to Hold Close:

- Regular church attendance isn't about checking a box - it's about creating a rhythm of peace and connection in your life

- Retreats and conferences can be powerful turning points in your healing journey

- Serving others through church programs can help shift your focus and bring unexpected peace

- Small groups and Bible studies provide safe spaces to grow in both faith and understanding

- Every step you take toward involvement is a step toward healing - no matter how small it might seem

The beautiful way to feel God's love in action is to connect with a Christian community. It reminds you that faith isn't supposed to be something you keep to yourself but something you share and grow with in relationship with others.

These connections encourage and bring a feeling of belonging, whether you're offering or receiving support or spending time with people who share your beliefs. There is a family of Christians within your church and community that wants to help you as you help them. Immerse yourself in your church community even if it doesn't feel easy yet. As you take each step, you connect deeper with others and grow closer to God.

Chapter 8: Dietary Adjustments and Mental Health

This chapter may make you feel uncomfortable. Very uncomfortable. I've done a lot of personal study on food, and I've experienced incredible physical and mental healing with it. In fact, I would say that 75% of my results have come from what I'm going to share with you about food.

I'm no nutritionist, so seek professional advice in regard to food, but I will share what's worked for me.

There's no two ways about it: what you eat really does affect your mental health. **Significantly.** In fact, the impact of food on mental health is far greater than most healthcare professionals even realize. Even worse, most are willing to argue against it and give you a prescription instead.

What I am going to tell you is simple, but not easy. Food is something I personally battle with every day, even though I know how dramatically it affects my mental health.

Why?

Because what's best for me isn't what I want, and the sugar demon has a deep hold on me. It's not the sugar demon you might imagine, either. I don't eat ice cream, chocolate, or candy.

I'll be honest with you: I feel best on a strict, dairy-free, caffeine-free carnivore diet. It cleared up a lot of my anxiety and has lifted some pretty deep periods of depression. I keep it simple by eating all different meats, but mostly red meat, sugar-free bacon, butter, and eggs. Like I said: Simple, but not easy. Carbohydrates, colloquially known as carbs, destroy my mental health. I don't know why, but I do know that not having them makes me feel better than I could have imagined.

I highly recommend watching Kelly Hogan's YouTube channel, myzerocarblife, if you want to learn more about it from a wonderful

Christian woman. One episode that stood out to me most is her interview with Brett Lloyd, the Thankful Carnivore. The episode is called *'Zero Carb "The Happiness Episode" with Kelly Hogan and Brett Lloyd.'* Brett talks about his battle with crippling depression, anger, and anxiety and how the carnivore diet healed it completely. Kelly's channel is a fantastic resource filled with personal stories, client results, and advice.

For some excellent interviews and anecdotes, look at Dave Mac's channel, No Carb Life (@zerocarb). The healings experienced by everyday people are truly remarkable.

There is a very good reason that the carnivore community call the effects of eating that way 'zero-carb zen'. Unless you've experienced it, describing the feeling is impossible. Most people feel like a weight and brain fog have been lifted from them, and very quickly. If there's no medical reason restricting you, I would highly suggest trying a strict carnivore diet for at least 30 days.

Second to carnivore, I feel best on whole food keto (without the keto treats) or low-carb Paleo.

Paleo focuses on whole, unprocessed foods like meats, seafood, fruits, vegetables, nuts, and seeds, which are rich in nutrients and free from artificial additives. The goal is to avoid foods that are modern inventions and could contribute to inflammation or poor health.

What to eat on the Paleo diet:

- **Meats:** Grass-fed beef, chicken, turkey, pork, and other lean meats.
- **Fish and seafood:** Wild-caught fish like salmon, mackerel, and tuna.
- **Fruits and vegetables:** Fresh, unprocessed varieties of fruits and vegetables, especially non-starchy ones.
- **Nuts and seeds:** Almonds, walnuts, chia seeds, flaxseeds, and other unsweetened varieties.
- **Healthy fats:** Avocados, olive oil, coconut oil, and animal fats.

What to avoid on the Paleo diet:

- **Grains**: All grains, including wheat, rice, oats, barley, and corn.
- **Dairy:** Milk, cheese, yogurt, and other dairy products.
- **Legumes:** Beans, lentils, peas, and peanuts.
- **Processed foods:** Packaged snacks, sugary treats, and other heavily processed foods.
- **Refined sugars:** Cane sugar, high-fructose corn syrup, and other artificial sweeteners.
- **Vegetable oils:** Soy, sunflower, canola, and other highly processed vegetable oils.
- **Alcohol:** All alcohol is forbidden on the Paleo diet.

The idea behind the Paleo diet is to focus on foods that are nutrient-dense, promote overall health, and are free from artificial ingredients or processing, while avoiding foods that could negatively impact your health due to their modern origins.

The Effects of Caffeine

You may have noticed I mentioned that I went caffeine-free. As a self-proclaimed coffee snob, this was one of the hardest changes for me to make. I had to wean myself off caffeine very slowly because the withdrawal symptoms were brutal. The headaches were severe enough, but the debilitating leg cramps I experienced—lasting for months—were even worse. Not even magnesium or electrolyte supplements seemed to help.

Despite the challenges, giving up caffeine significantly reduced my anxiety. That doesn't mean I've given up coffee entirely—I've just switched to high-quality, Swiss Water process decaffeinated coffee. It's a work in progress, as I'm also transitioning from milk-based coffee to black coffee to reduce dairy, which hasn't been kind to my weight during early menopause.

If you decide to give up caffeine, take it slow. Reduce your intake by about 10% at a time. I blend my coffee beans by hand to adjust the ratio, but your approach will depend on how you prepare your coffee. Most people will defend their coffee habit above nearly anything else. It's not until you drop it, that you realize you feel better and have more energy without it.

This advice also applies to tea—opt for decaffeinated versions or naturally caffeine-free options like vanilla rooibos. It's a tough journey, but it's absolutely doable with patience and the right strategy.

As Christians, we often want to connect our faith to practical portions of our daily lives. Look at your diet through a faith lens and you'll see that it does more than strengthen your body—it can improve your mood in surprising ways.

By approaching nutrition with care and intention, you can discover how it plays a role in your emotional balance and overall health. With God's guidance, even simple choices around food can feel like a meaningful step toward a healthier, more peaceful life.

Understanding the Mental Health Benefits of Nutritional Changes

It's fascinating to see how simple shifts in what you eat can strengthen not just your body but also your emotional well-being. For example, certain vitamins and minerals, like B vitamins, magnesium, and zinc, play a big role in how your brain functions. They affect your mood and energy, making them especially important if you're dealing with anxiety or depression. Paying attention to these nutrients is one way to care for the body God has entrusted to you.

The simplest way to support your mental health is by choosing foods that reduce inflammation. Low-inflammation foods keep your blood sugar stable. Keeping your blood sugar stable can make a big difference in how you feel emotionally. When your blood sugar levels swing too high or too low, it can lead to irritability and anxiety. This is where a zero-carb or keto diet shines. This kind of diet significantly reduces the blood sugar spikes of a standard diet. That equals a stable mood and constant energy without the ups and downs caused by sugar/carb spikes.

Your gut health also influences how you feel emotionally. Researchers are discovering exciting new insights into how the bacteria in your gut can influence your mood. Enjoying clean foods, especially fermented foods, can support your gut health, and that will positively impact your mental well-being. If in doubt, buy only whole foods and avoid gluten and grains.

If going zero carb or keto feels a little too extreme initially, read through the book, Glucose Revolution by Jessie Inchauspé (https://www.glucosegoddess.com/). Jessie shares simple and doable techniques to smooth out your blood sugar spikes. This is a great first step to healing from anxiety. By taking small, intentional steps in your diet, you're nurturing the whole person God created you to be.

The Role of Nutritional Deficiencies in Mental Health

It's easy to forget how important nutrition is for our mental health. Lack of essential nutrients, such as vitamins and minerals, significantly impacts mental health, often exacerbating symptoms of anxiety and depression. Most of the time, we fail to understand or recognize the obvious correlation between what we consume and our mental state.

Think of the brain's functioning when critical nutrients are absent. Folate and B12 vitamins help create the mood-regulating neurotransmitters, and minerals like magnesium and zinc are essential to brain function and stress regulation. These deficits disrupt the balance necessary for maintaining mental health and increase the feelings of anxiety and depression. Research suggests that when these nutrients are lacking, you might notice your symptoms getting worse. This highlights how important it is to have a diet that helps replenish these key components.

However, most people have no idea that if they're lacking these nutrients, it can cause anxiety and depression. The abundance of cheap, processed foods devoid of nutritional value has made it difficult for many to attain the vitamins and minerals necessary for optimal mental health. As a result, people may mistakenly attribute symptoms of mental health issues to stress or life circumstances instead of an underlying nutritional deficiency.

When you're moving toward better mental health through faith, aligning dietary adjustments with God's provision makes sense. After all, He provided us with the perfect foods for humans long before industrialization, the government, and big food companies—which are all bought and paid for—took over and decided to tell us what they think is best for us.

Faith-integrated nutrition recognizes God's gift of nature's bounty and encourages us to view food as a blessing rather than just sustenance. By turning to whole foods—meats, fruits, and vegetables—and seeing them as part of God's provision, individuals can nourish not only their bodies but also support spiritual growth. It's important to allow your faith to guide decisions concerning nutrition so you can create harmony between your dietary choices and spiritual beliefs. When you eat mindfully, acknowledging the nourishment provided by God, you develop appreciation and intentionality in every meal.

For the purpose of discussing nutritional deficiencies, the Christian concept of the body being a temple can help you understand how nutrition affects anxiety. When you regard your body as a temple of God, you'll understand the need to feed the body properly. This mindset empowers us to commit to healthier dietary practices not out of obligation but reverence. Nourishing the body with the required nutrients becomes a form of worship and respect for yourself and for God, resulting in improved mental health and a closer spiritual connection.

If you are starting with a holistic approach to mental well-being, you can begin with identifying what your personal dietary needs are. It's important to take time to have an honest look at your current eating habits and see where you may need to pay attention. Be truthful with yourself. Even I find it difficult at times to be honest with myself about food because it has such a deep emotional connection. If you're unsure where your nutrition is lacking, consulting a healthcare provider or nutritionist can help you pin down the nutrients that are missing for you. They will let you know which vitamins and minerals you're lacking and will help you include these in your diet with the right foods. If that option is unaffordable at the moment, consider tracking what you eat for a few days in an app called Chronometer. It will show you which nutrient targets you are meeting and which ones you aren't.

It doesn't have to feel like you are adjusting your whole diet. Begin by adding more nutrient-rich foods to your day, gradually. For instance, you could substitute sugary snacks for nuts or low-sugar fruits like berries, and add more eggs and red meat to give you almost every nutrient you need. These small changes can add up over time, creating sustainable habits. Be patient with yourself. Progress doesn't happen overnight, but those steady steps reflect the Christian value of perseverance.

One thing I can highly recommend doing is logging your food on an app called Chronometer for a while. The reason I suggest this is because the free version of Chronometer tracks all of your micronutrients, not just your food. By doing this for a week or so, you'll soon see the gaps in your nutrition. From there, you can research the foods you need to add to help you balance your diet correctly. Use it until you find the foods that support your body and make you feel good psychologically.

You don't have to make these changes alone. Lean on your community for support. An accountability partner from your church can help you stay committed while providing encouragement. Telling them details of your progress, challenges, and successes can make the process of getting healthier feel less isolating. If diet is something you'd prefer to keep private, consider joining an online group for support with your chosen direction.

Anti-Inflammatory Foods and Their Mental Health Benefits

Recent research reveals the link between inflammation and mental health and suggests that eating anti-inflammatory foods is far more important for helping to maintain emotional stability than previously thought. Inflammation, something rarely considered by health professionals, can heavily affect your mood and how you interact with the world around you. In numerous interviews I've watched, most people didn't comprehend the mental impact of inflammation until they transitioned to a keto or carnivore diet and experienced a reduction in 'brain fog.' Interviewees report feeling a clarity in their mind they've never experienced before. You can reduce the inflammation and create a healthy foundation for better mental health by making some thoughtful dietary choices.

Anti-inflammatory foods, such as meat, eggs, salmon, walnuts, spinach, blueberries, and strawberries, work by calming the body's immune response. However, it's important to understand that foods like spinach and kale are high in oxalates. High oxalate foods can cause kidney stones and other health issues. Lower oxalate vegetables include arugula, avocado, bok choy, cabbage, cauliflower, cilantro, cucumber, garlic, lettuce, mushrooms, onions, red bell pepper, and green peas. These nutrient-packed options don't just nourish your body—they support a balanced mind, offering a natural way to stabilize mood and boost energy. Low oxalate foods can have big effects on your emotional and physical health.

This transition can feel achievable if you change your diet slowly. You may begin by adding another serving of meat and low-carb/low-oxalate vegetables to your meals or replacing sugary drinks with unsweetened black coffee or tea. It's the small changes that can become lasting habits over time.

Understanding the Gut-Brain Connection

Very few people, including medical professionals, understand how gut health affects mental health. Recently, scientific research from Stanford has uncovered a strong link between your gut and your brain, also known as the 'gut-brain axis.' A healthy gut microbiome (the trillions of bacteria that make up your digestive system) can make a huge difference in your mood and anxiety levels. This is an important connection for you to understand. For mental health challenges like anxiety or depression, when you understand the gut-brain relationship, you'll discover new ways to heal.

In other words, your gut doesn't just help with the digestion of food; it actually helps produce neurotransmitters such as serotonin and dopamine, which help regulate your mood. Some of these neurotransmitter levels can become imbalanced, leading to mental health issues. A balanced gut microbiome may aid in the more efficient production of these chemicals, consequently reducing anxiety and enhancing mood. According to studies, people with a diverse, balanced gut have fewer symptoms of anxiety and depression.

Clean eating and probiotics emerge as important components in maintaining gut health. Clean eating refers to consuming whole, unprocessed foods that provide natural nourishment. Probiotics introduce live beneficial bacteria into your system. You can find these in fermented foods like yogurt, kefir, sauerkraut, and kimchi. Including these foods in your diet can help maintain a robust microbiome, as a result supporting your mental well-being. However, a review of seven randomized control trials has shown that there is no evidence that probiotics improve the intestinal microbiota of healthy people. (Source: Dr. Robert Kiltz). The important word there is healthy people. If your diet isn't healthy, then there could be some benefit to including fermented foods until you heal.

As a Christian seeking a holistic approach to mental health, you can integrate scriptural wisdom into your dietary choices to encourage personal accountability and spiritual alignment. Scripture encourages you to care for your body, seeing it as a temple of God. By aligning your dietary habits with biblical principles, you can embrace a more intentional lifestyle. Proverbs 23:2 warns against gluttony, while 1 Corinthians 10:31 reminds you to do everything for God's glory. These verses can inspire mindfulness in your dietary decisions, encouraging a balance that honors your body as a vessel of God's presence.

Intertwining scientific insights with faith-based perspectives enriches your well-being. While science explains the mechanisms of gut health's impact on mental health, your faith offers a framework for finding meaning and purpose in this knowledge. Faith and science aren't mutually exclusive; instead, they complement each other, giving you a broader understanding of health and wellness. Embracing this dual perspective allows you to approach your mental health with both evidence-based strategies and spiritual guidance.

Bringing together diet, science, and faith gives you some helpful tools to help you reach a balanced sense of well-being. Science breaks down how things work, and your faith adds meaning to it all. Finding a good balance is key, and leaning on your faith can help you make choices that will improve your mind, body, and spirit.

Steps to Integrate Dietary Changes

Improving your mental health through diet involves a structured and mindful approach. It starts with understanding your specific dietary needs. You need to be aware of any nutritional deficiencies you may have. These deficiencies can manifest as fatigue, mood swings, or long-term depression, which can exacerbate anxiety. Understanding exactly what you're missing in your diet can be tricky, so identifying these gaps might involve a bit of introspection about your daily dietary habits. In some cases, you might need to consult a professional to help determine what's lacking.

Once you understand your eating needs, it's crucial to make gradual changes. If you decide on a carnivore or keto diet, research low/zero-carb doctors on YouTube to understand what to expect in the first few weeks of your new diet. Some of my favorites are Dr. Anthony Chaffee, Dr. Ken Berry, Dr. Robert Kiltz, Professor Bart Kay, and Dr. Philip Ovadia.

Going from a standard Western diet to a healthy one can cause your body to react in different ways. It's important to know how to address any issues that pop up, as well as what's normal and what isn't.

If you're thinking about starting with a paleo protocol, the best book is *It Starts with Food: Discover the Whole30 and Change Your Life in Unexpected Ways* by Dallas and Melissa Hartwig. If you are looking for Paleo recipes, *Fast Food for Busy Families: More Than 100 Quick and Easy Paleo Recipes* by Pete Evans, an Australian chef, is fantastic.

Patience is crucial for any significant change. It's a Christian virtue that is very much needed when making major dietary changes. I'm not going to say it isn't challenging. My diet is something I still struggle with. Start with small steps, such as adding more red meat and low-carb fruits and vegetables to your meals while reducing your sugar intake. These incremental changes will help keep you consistent, and your body will have time to adjust to the new routine so you'll find it easier to stick to.

Finding support through online communities can be incredibly helpful if you're exploring a specific diet. If you're looking for groups led by influencers or true enthusiasts of a certain dietary approach, platforms like YouTube, Facebook, or Instagram are great ways to find them. Before you join a group, check out the leaders' qualifications, and make sure that the group includes input from medical professionals to help you get balanced and safe guidance.

If you're interested in the carnivore diet, Kelly Hogan, who runs My Zero Carb Life (myzerocarblife.com), is absolutely amazing. Her community offers support, inspiration, and practical advice rooted in her own journey with the diet. Her Christian viewpoint will make you comfortable that your faith is going to be respected. Kelly's group is a welcoming space for those seeking encouragement outside of traditional church groups.

Praying for guidance is another essential spiritual anchor during dietary transitions. Prayer offers you a space for reflection and opens your heart to divine assistance and wisdom. It reminds you of your reliance on God's strength and the peace that comes from surrendering your struggle to Him. This practice is not only about seeking help but also about finding inspiration and motivation to stay committed to your new dietary path. Incorporating prayer into your mealtimes, thanking God for the nourishing food, and asking for His continued guidance can become a powerful habit, reinforcing the connection between nutrition and spiritual wellness.

When you're making these dietary changes, be open to learning and adapting. Sometimes what works for one person doesn't work for you. Flexibility is key. If you do not see a difference after certain changes, visit a nutritionist and see what else you can do to improve your mood and energy levels. This journey is very personal, and so tuning into your body and trusting your instincts will help you make choices that are right for you. Knowing where your food comes from, how it affects your body, and its nutritional value will help you make better choices.

Insights and Implications

A key part of managing your anxiety, and even depression, is addressing nutritional deficiencies. The more you recognize the gaps in your diet and make conscious changes, the more you will nourish your body and mind. Professionals and online communities can assist you in taking small, life-changing steps to improve emotional well-being. But remember, caring for your body is much more than physical—it's a spiritual act honoring the gift of health God has given you.

"Breathe darling. This is just a chapter. It's not your whole story."

~ S.C. Lourie ~

Chapter 9: Balancing Faith and Emotional Struggles

Being a Christian and living with anxiety is like having your feet standing in two worlds at once—one in faith and one in fear. You want to trust in God, but you're experiencing racing thoughts and anxious feelings, which you might feel are 'unGodly'.

Most people face an inner clash since they know God leads with goodness and sovereignty, yet their minds continually think about worst-case outcomes. Your anxiety might lead you to question both the strength of your faith and the ethicalness of using medication when you strive to trust God's healing abilities.

Being a Christian doesn't make you immune to emotional struggles. Consider Elijah, who was so depressed that he cried out to God to end his life. The heroes of our Bible remind us that just because we have faith doesn't mean we won't experience emotional battles.

This chapter explores the ways the Word of God addresses both the spiritual and emotional, while modern anxiety treatment supports (rather than conflicts with) Christian beliefs. Both prayer and practical tools can be integrated together. God provides answers to your prayers by providing counseling services as well as food supplies, medications, and alternative coping mechanisms.

Identifying Conflicts Between Emotions and Religious Teachings

Understanding the balance between your faith and emotions is like navigating a delicate situation, where each step requires both wisdom and grace. A big part of healing is learning that your emotions are valid experiences that don't have to be at war with your faith. The more you understand your emotions as being part of your human experience, the more you'll understand yourself. Many religious communities overlook this, believing that emotions indicate spiritual weakness. But when you see your emotions as God-given, you can welcome them and work with them without fear of judgment.

It's possible to encounter some expectations from others, or even from yourself, that are a bit unrealistic. It's common to feel a little guilty when you don't meet those expectations. This guilt usually comes from historical interpretations of religious teachings. They often promote ideals of unwavering faith and emotional stoicism—ideals that don't really apply in the modern world.

Humans have grown emotionally in the past century, and we are more inclined to feel our feelings rather than hide them. When you suffer from anxiety, depression, or any other emotional challenge, the pressure to seem like you're always keeping your faith constant, without doubt or distress, can make you feel like you're not good enough. It is important for your faith to practice emotional authenticity. If you can find strength in being vulnerable and accept that you have flaws, you can explore the depth of your relationship with God in an honest way.

Stereotypes about faith and emotional struggles may also hinder your personal growth and the support you receive from your community. Religious stereotypes may also get in the way of your personal growth. Often religion has associated emotional struggles with a lack of faith or commitment and silences those who struggle with their mental health. You can start by facilitating open conversations and creating safe spaces to talk about what struggles you are facing, helping stomp out stigma. This sets you and others up for acceptance and empathy so that you can create a supportive network for spiritual growth with mental well-being.

I want to speak to that tender place in your heart where guilt and faith cross paths. Have you felt that feeling—the one that says, 'I'm just not good enough for God's expectations'? Am I somehow just failing Him?' Maybe you've lain awake at night, wondering if a 'real' Christian would struggle like this or if seeking help means you're not trusting God enough.

Can I share something with you? That guilt you're carrying wasn't meant to be part of your story. Guilt can muffle your voice and keep you from reaching out—whether to God, to others, or to the help He may have placed in your path. But here's the beautiful truth: when you find the courage to be real about your struggles, something remarkable happens.

When you decide to be honest about your struggles with anxiety, you're not only helping yourself heal, but you're also helping others heal too. You're creating a sacred space for others to whisper, "Me too." Isn't that just our God? He uses our darkest struggles to create bridges that help others find their way to healing as well. It's not weakness to be real and open. It's called being human. It's one of the most powerful ways you can show God's grace at work in your life.

Acknowledging your emotions doesn't mean letting them control you. Instead, accept them as signals, guiding you to areas in need of reflection and spiritual growth. Emotions can help you engage in more meaningful conversations with God. When you accept this coexistence, you take care of both your faith and all the emotions that come along with it.

Working toward being true to yourself while navigating unrealistic expectations of faith can be tough, but it's also fulfilling. It encourages honesty with your beliefs, giving you the space to explore and deal with tough emotions without the worry of feeling insincere in your faith. This transforms how you experience faith, making it more about relationships and less about just showing up. As you embrace authenticity, you can find renewed strength in your spiritual walk, gaining resilience to face life's trials.

Challenging stereotypes about faith and emotions is essential for growth. When you and your church community confront these stereotypes, you create environments where people can connect deeply, knowing their true selves are seen and valued. This shift helps build congregations that actively support each other's healing, offering comfort and companionship to those facing emotional struggles.

Unchecked guilt often turns into shame, which can create huge blocks to healing. Having an open conversation about guilt and its impact on your faith can help you sort out any unhealthy links between your feelings and your beliefs. This allows for a conversation to happen, encouraging understanding and replacing self-criticism with kindness and compassion, which helps build a culture of support and growth.

Crafting Your Personal Action Plan

When you balance your faith and emotional struggles, starting with a personalized approach is essential. You experience faith and mental health in your own unique way, so blending these elements into your daily life is necessary for building resilience. By creating a customized plan that combines your faith practices with mental health strategies, you can build up your inner strength. It's important to bring together your spiritual beliefs and your emotional needs. Ensure they work together harmoniously instead of clashing.

The first thing I recommend is to take some time to find out what spiritual practices bring you peace and what mental health tools make you feel better. Maybe you find comfort in prayer and meditation, or you might feel that journaling or talking to a professional works better for you. Don't force yourself into a rigid routine—choose practices that resonate with you personally. By tailoring a path to your needs, you can actively participate in your emotional wellness.

Once your personalized approach is in place, actively participating in it becomes easier. When you create your plan, you naturally feel more responsible for following through. This accountability encourages consistent engagement, reinforcing your commitment to emotional health. Managing your emotional challenges alongside faith-based practices then becomes a meaningful pursuit of well-being, rather than a burden.

Your emotional and spiritual needs will change as your life changes. You may need to try different practices depending on your healing stage. It may be that what works for you today won't work for you tomorrow. Be open to new ways of healing that can meet your current needs.

Imagine you're adding mindfulness and box breathing to your prayer time, and it relaxes your mind and keeps you calm for the day. Or you can combine reading scripture with gratitude journaling to get you to think about the positive things in your life based on ideas from the Bible. The possibilities are endless, and exploring them can help you adapt and grow.

Combining faith and mental wellness strategies that you love will give you a balanced outlook on life. When these two things coexist in harmony, they help each other and form a solid base for your total well-being. Leaning on your faith can keep you hopeful and purposeful, even in the worst of times.

Consider adding practices like weekly devotional readings. Weekly isn't quite as overwhelming as daily when you already have so much going on. *From Worry to Worship: A 52-Week Devotional Bible Study for Anxiety* is the matching devotional to this book making it perfect for this practice. Daily, you could add a few minutes of breathwork or visualization to your routine. These simple habits bridge the gap between spiritual nourishment and emotional stability, helping you face life's challenges with grace and composure.

A good starting point is to craft your personal action plan. Define what you want to achieve emotionally and spiritually and set clear objectives. Next, determine which practices will align with these goals. It's not about how many times you go to church per week or how often you pray; it's about consistency. Make sure to keep track of what works for you and modify your plan as you go. Your plan should be adaptable as it can change over time.

By embracing flexibility, you can keep your plans sustainable in the long term. If you stick to a single practice rigidly, you might get bored or frustrated or even burn out if it becomes too overwhelming. Think of your plan as a living one, changing with the changing circumstances. This flexibility allows you to remain resilient and flexible during life's ups and downs, thanks to your open mindset.

Utilizing Community Support

Your church or faith-based community is probably more than just a place to worship for you. It's a support system that gives you community, belonging, and spiritual and emotional backup. Being active in your church can help you feel connected and at peace.

A supportive Christian community surrounds you with people who are like-minded and have similar beliefs. This shared foundation gives you a kind of understanding that you may not have elsewhere. The fundamental teachings of Christianity remind you to love and support one another. In this way, close-knit church communities are perfect for those needing emotional healing. Its members come together and offer empathy and compassion, which can help minimize the sense of isolation that might be a result of battling emotional challenges.

It becomes a powerful act of self-validation when you share your personal struggles within your community. Sharing what you worry about, what scares you, and what gets you down can help you find others who have gone down that path. This kind of sharing often becomes purifying. The more people who hear your story, the more encouraging they become for you and for one another. This strengthens everyone's faith and will help you feel supported. This can reassure you and help you believe more strongly in a compassionate and supportive God.

The collective nature of faith-based communities offers countless opportunities for your spiritual and emotional growth. Joining small groups, Bible studies, or volunteering activities can help you deepen your faith while also nurturing your emotional health. These group efforts allow you to explore new facets of your spirituality and discover methods for emotional self-care. By looking out for one another and pooling resources, you and your community members can learn coping strategies and practical ways to manage mental health.

Outside of your church options, anxiety support groups can offer valuable insights and opportunities for growth. They are usually available both online and offline if you feel you need extra support to heal. These sessions are run by trained therapists who specialize in different aspects of anxiety or depression. You can heal a lot yourself, especially when you make the adjustments suggested in this book, but sometimes you need deeper-level healing.

For these benefits to truly take root, approach community support with an open and willing heart. Actively participating and engaging with others requires a willingness to be vulnerable—to both give and receive help. Building authentic relationships necessitates commitment and trust, but the rewards can enrich your life immeasurably.

It is important to draw on community support, but it is equally important to put yourself on a schedule that includes some time with yourself and God. Your community involvement should add to, not take the place of, your individual faith practices. And it's a great way to strike a balance between group participation and personal reflection while approaching your spiritual and emotional challenges holistically.

Creating Rituals for Connecting to God

Rituals can be important for grounding yourself in the middle of your daily activities. They support mindfulness, emotional wellness, and faith. These techniques help you reset yourself and provide a concrete approach to interact with your emotional needs as well as your spiritual beliefs. Here are some common and unique ideas for rituals you can use to connect with God:

- a morning prayer
- an evening meditation
- lighting a candle and focusing on God
- scripture meditation, where you choose a passage from the Bible and meditate on it
- using a daily devotional
- a walking prayer where you go for a walk and talk to God
- evening confession where you share with God your struggles and ask for
- forgiveness (along with forgiving yourself)
- scripture doodling where you draw a passage you've read in the Bible
- a space blessing where you bless different parts of your home

You may come up with your own ideas as well. The beauty of rituals is in their simplicity. Only act on a ritual that connects you to God or Jesus and doesn't make you feel overwhelmed. The first step to incorporating these ideas into your daily life is to start small. Pick out one or two practices that really speak to you right now. Setting specific times each day to do these rituals might be helpful until it's second nature. This routine will become solid, and you'll realize you have a different approach to daily stresses. You'll be less reactive, more reflective, and more aligned with your spiritual and emotional goals.

By setting up daily practices on purpose, you're taking care of your emotional well-being. These are simple practices, but they create an environment where your emotional care meets your faith. Building up a couple of daily rituals is like creating a space with a sanctuary within. They become a place to go to replenish your spirit and emotions. These rituals are comforting for people dealing with anxiety, depression, or any other emotional stressor. They help you stay balanced on both your faith and emotional health sides of the scale.

When prayer is woven into personal reflection, you are creating the space in your mind for emotional processing. Prayer is not only talking to your Creator; it is also talking to yourself. In these moments, you vocalize your fears, your hopes, your anxieties, and your joys. You're letting them be seen and understood. By combining prayer and reflection, you engage in self-discovery, recognizing and overcoming emotional challenges while maintaining your connection to your faith.

Rituals do not necessarily mean lengthy or complex practices. They can be as simple as a short walk while reciting affirmations, writing a daily gratitude list, or sitting quietly with a few deep breaths before a meal. What really matters is the intention behind the ritual—it's all about making a conscious choice to weave spirituality and emotional care into your daily routine. This helps you to lighten your load, bringing you some clarity and calm even when things get a bit hectic.

Not only do these routines help your well-being, but they have ripples; they impact your relationships, your life-work balance, and your overall happiness. Internal peace is an essential ingredient to your ability to respond to external challenges.

Creating rituals for connection helps bridge the gap between your faith and emotional health. It's such a simple thing to light a candle during prayer or to use a gratitude jar at home, but it is a powerful blend of spirituality and mindfulness. These rituals can help you create a peaceful environment where you can heal emotionally in the comfort of your home.

These intentional practices really show how powerful it can be to blend spirituality with taking care of our emotions. These rituals remind you that healing and growth are ongoing processes. They take time and commitment. As these routines become a part of your everyday life, they will soon transform from 'tasks' to something you cherish, as you notice how they rejuvenate your soul and mind.

Flexibility in Your Christian Practices

When working through the difficult emotions of anxiety or depression, it is important to have flexibility in how you practice your faith. By being flexible, you can create sustainable habits that support your emotional as well as your spiritual well-being. By adjusting how you practice your faith based on what's going on in your life, you are creating an environment where both your spirit and mind can thrive.

Take, for instance, the idea of prayer. Traditionally associated with specific times spent kneeling beside your bed or in church, prayer can transform into a continuous dialogue with God throughout your day. This kind of adaptability lets you talk with Him whenever you're feeling overwhelmed, providing comfort whenever you need it. Sustainable faith practices focus on how your faith can seamlessly blend into your everyday life, rather than just perfect attendance at church services or following strict routines. When you're feeling down or anxious, sometimes sitting quietly and simply being present with God can be as powerful as lengthy prayers.

Life isn't predictable, and it's not always best for you to stick to the traditional religious practices, especially in times of tumult. Practices can be adapted to help you with emotional resilience. As an example, if you're reading scripture, rather than tackling big chapters, maybe you could read smaller ones that speak directly to the struggles you're facing in your life right now. These practices become personalized, allowing you to hear what feeds your soul at those times. Let's say that going to church is too overwhelming for you because of social anxiety; virtual services or listening to sermons online are an alternative way to stay connected without the additional stress.

Like any other aspect of life, growth and evolution are beneficial for faith. The more you mature, the more you understand and relate to God. You should allow your faith to naturally develop, as it will manifest differently at different stages of your life. It's all about looking back at how much you've achieved and realizing that your future holds even more opportunities for growth. Change shouldn't be something to fear. Instead, it's something to embrace with an open heart. Take a moment to reflect on the beginnings of your faith. Some of the beliefs you held back then may have evolved and deepened as you've matured and discovered new insights. This is a perfectly normal and healthy progression!

Having adaptable approaches to your faith supports long-term emotional balance. Faith is not something that binds you to the rules; it should be there with you 24/7. You can seamlessly integrate Christian teachings like contemplation and reflection with your new practices, such as meditation or mindfulness. You need to focus on the methods that will help you calm your mind and reduce anxiety. It's okay to merge the old with the new when it comes to modernizing your faith. Modern techniques are proven to reduce anxiety, so feel free to incorporate them into your religion in a way that works for you.

The concept of flexibility in faith isn't so much about abandoning the established rituals but about enriching them to make sense in your life. A devotional that shines a light on anxiety specifically, can be the perfect relief and upliftment when you need it the most by connecting you to scripture. Take a look at *From Worry to Worship: A 52-Week Devotional Bible Study for Anxiety* and see if it resonates with you. These adjustments keep the sacredness and importance of your practices intact. They're thoughtful changes that help ensure your faith continues to be a source of strength in your life.

Let me tell you about the story of Phil, a man who was very dedicated to his church community. Phil suddenly faced some tough times that caused him to be filled with anxiety. Instead of helping him relax, he found that going to weekly Bible study was more stressful for him. So, to take in the material in more manageable chunks, he decided to set up private study sessions at his house. This change enabled him to spend time with the Bible in a way that helped protect his emotional state.

How you define community involvement also needs to be flexible. You don't necessarily need to be physically present. It can include using virtual meetups, encouraging others online, donating money, blogging, or helping Christian volunteer agencies remotely. This broadens your perspective and enables you to control your emotional fluctuations.

The main thing to learn here is that when you are flexible in your faith, you show up for God and yourself in a real way. It allows you to stand firm in your beliefs while extending yourself grace in focusing on your well-being. Faith should never be a burden to practice when it's woven into your life thoughtfully. Instead, it transforms into a stable and unwavering presence that guides you through life.

Wisdom for Moving Ahead

Our emotions become an essential part of our spiritual growth when we embrace them as God-given. When you don't judge your feelings, you're creating a space where emotional struggles don't have to be a sign that you have weak faith but a chance to grow and to connect. We've previously discussed how the authenticity of faith can alleviate feelings of guilt and shame. By sharing your story openly, you are challenging stereotypes. This opens the way for a more accepting and empathetic community.

Creating your own personal action plans bridges the gap between faith and mental well-being and helps you find practices that work for you. It's all about experimenting with different methods so that you adapt to change. These personalized strategies can turn dealing with emotional challenges into something meaningful instead of being a burden.

By being flexible in faith practice, you inadvertently make sure that your faith continues to support and sustain you through the difficulties of life. When you merge your spiritual beliefs with emotional care to facilitate your own holistic healing, you come closer to God.

*"We just need to be
kinder to ourselves.
If we treated ourselves
the way we treated
our best friend,
can you imagine how much
better off we would be?"*

~ Meghan Markle ~

Chapter 10: Empathy and Emotional Connection

Empathy and emotional connection are part of how we relate to others and heal. It enables people to comprehend and experience the emotions of others. To demonstrate empathy means both understanding what another person feels and offering compassionate assistance.

Relationships can become even better when you understand and feel a person's emotions. Practicing empathy isn't just about growing our relationships with others; it's also an environment for emotional recovery. Empathy connects us from feelings of anxiety, depression, fear, or worry to a place of understanding and support for others. It invites us into a community of individuals who share emotions and lighten each other's loads.

Using Empathy to Build Stronger Relationships

Empathy drives meaningful connections, and it forms the foundation of emotional healing. At its heart, empathy begins with active listening. This makes others feel heard and validated. You'll find that when someone actually listens without judgment, it allows you to feel safe to share your vulnerabilities. Sometimes just knowing that someone cares to listen can make all the difference in the world.

Active listening is not just hearing words; it is being fully present with the person whose words you are hearing. It's about looking in someone's eyes, nodding, and providing that soft, verbal affirmation, like, "I hear you," or "I'm with you." Such small things are indicative of you caring about how that person feels. You're creating a safe environment that allows the person to be vulnerable with you. Deep listening of this kind builds trust and a foundation for more intimate connections—both of which are needed for emotional healing. By becoming an active listener, you'll find others naturally doing the same with you.

Empathy goes way beyond mere listening. It involves putting ourselves in the shoes of the other person and feeling what they are feeling from their point of reference. This imaginative leap strengthens relational bonds and tears down barriers traditionally built by anxiety or depression. Consider the biblical principle of *"Love your neighbor as yourself,"* which discusses true empathy. This passage is directing us to look upon others' feelings from a point of view of understanding and compassion.

Empathy is an essential part of living a Christ-like life, as shown in Colossians 3:12. *"Therefore, as God's chosen people, holy and dearly loved, clothe yourselves with compassion, kindness, humility, gentleness, and patience."*

By virtue of us putting ourselves in another's position, we get to know more about their struggles, their fears, and their joys. Seeing the world from another's perspective is a practice that creates true understanding. It is the process that builds bridges between individuals. We can then provide and receive helpful support. This builds up the relationship and aids in emotional healing. Taking the time to appreciate what someone else is experiencing will honor someone's story, and it will affirm their humanity.

Words are not at all the only way to express empathy; it can also be felt through actions. Verbal and nonverbal expressions of empathy, like speaking a kind word or showing a supportive gesture, are most important in relationship dynamics. It doesn't take much to show you care: a simple smile, a reassuring touch on the shoulder, or a thoughtful note.

Empathy using these types of expressions creates a support system where people feel accepted and heard. Connection to community is necessary for our emotional resilience. It's through sharing experiences with empathy and creating these relationships that we feel part of a community. Healing anxiety heavily relies on connection.

Empathetic relationships can really help reduce feelings of loneliness. Empathy-based communities encourage individuals to share their burdens, thereby encouraging healing for everyone involved. The collective approach to empathy builds resilience, allowing us to tap into strength and support when it's needed most.

In empathetic group sessions, every participant engages in healing. Hearing the stories of others, building a sense of understanding, and sharing a foundation of hope illustrates how lives can transform when we come together. Each act of kindness will strengthen and enhance our community, bringing us together as one with a shared purpose.

If you want to learn empathy, begin by practicing active listening in conversations in your daily life with the aim of really understanding others. Rather than jumping to respond, see if you can't take a moment to truly hear what the other person has to say. Reflect back to them what you hear so they know that you understand them. Responding to them thoughtfully and validating their feelings is a wonderful way to build exceptional relationships. An open dialogue in your church community encourages building these networks and supportive group conversations where empathy can thrive and emotional healing occurs.

For Christians looking for holistic healing, empathizing closely reflects the vision of faith. Christ consciousness represents the essence of Jesus' teachings, showcasing compassion and understanding through action. Christians can enhance their spiritual lives by following His example to bring peace into their lives and discovering serenity through their capacity to give and receive compassion.

Sharing Personal Stories to Build Connection

When you're struggling with anxiety and are held within its grip, it can be challenging to put yourself out there. It's common to withdraw to varying degrees from family, friends, and your congregation. While you can heal from anxiety alone, it's better to use your situation to grow relationships and build connections.

Sharing your personal story is a lovely way to build personal connections and reduce the feeling of loneliness. By choosing to be vulnerable and share your story, you create an opportunity for meaningful and authentic conversations. Vulnerability, though often perceived as a weakness, strengthens bonds and relationships. This will help you transform your fear and anxiety into trust in God, others, and yourself.

Think about how relatable experiences shared through personal stories are. When someone bravely shares their story, it resonates deeply with many people, especially those who share a common faith, such as

Christians. These stories help people feel that healing isn't just a dream; it's something that can be reached together within a church community that cares for each other.

When you tell your personal story, you inspire hope and motivate others to keep going. But listening to how other people have worked through their anxiety will show you that there are lots of ways to heal.

These stories remind you and others of how strong we all can be when recovering from a tough time, especially when the burden is shared. Their stories verify that healing is not a universal process. There are many unique paths to healing and emotional recovery.

To make storytelling useful, you must listen to and validate the emotions of others. You strengthen trust and relationships when you recognize and acknowledge what another person is feeling. Listen sincerely and with empathy. This helps to break down barriers like mistrust or anxiety.

Storytelling isn't just about sharing events; it's about connecting emotionally. When you stay present, listen actively, and respond with kindness, you help create a safe space where vulnerability is met with understanding, not judgment. This is especially powerful in faith-based settings, where shared spiritual values can give personal stories even deeper meaning and help you find purpose in struggles.

You can show how vulnerability turns to strength via your personal story. When you're open about your experiences, it helps other people to be honest about theirs, and this cycle of trust and understanding continues. It aligns with biblical teachings for Christians, which emphasize compassion, love, and supporting each other in life.

To really make storytelling work, why not incorporate it into your group's regular activities, like workshops or discussion sessions? Every participant can feel safe to share as long as there are clear rules for respectful listening. This is a wonderful way to break emotional barriers and encourage trust so everyone can grow together.

Understanding Emotional Connection

As Christians, we have a duty to love and show compassion to each other. Empathy is showing others that you understand and respect how they feel. This creates trust, which is the foundation of any meaningful relationship. If people trust you, they feel comfortable enough to open up.

Before helping other people, though, it's essential to learn self-compassion. When I first began battling anxiety, my mind was filled with only negative thoughts. The voice inside my head was constantly criticizing me—telling me I wasn't enough, that I'd never make it, or that I was just too much of a mess. I know I'm not the only one who's felt that way. You've probably heard that voice too, whether it's whispering doubts or shouting insecurities.

But here's the thing: if we're constantly beating ourselves up, how are we ever supposed to show compassion to others? We can't pour from an empty cup. And when we don't show ourselves the same love and care that God shows us, it's challenging to extend that same grace to anyone else. It's like trying to comfort someone when you're wrapped up in your own pain. You can't assist someone if you're unable to assist yourself.

To have self-compassion, you need to treat yourself the way God treats you. Give yourself enough grace to show yourself love, forgiveness, and patience. God doesn't criticize you when you fall short, so why should you treat yourself that way? Instead, He loves you deeply. That's the kind of love we're called to show to ourselves.

Your critical inner voice will quieten when you practice self-compassion. Replace criticism with God's love and self-love. I remember a time when I was struggling to get through a really rough few weeks. I had to remind myself over and over, "God loves me, flaws and all. I'm allowed to be imperfect. I'm allowed to have tough days. That doesn't mean I'm a failure." Once I started talking to myself with kindness, I became more empathetic to others.

It's not easy to sit with our negative feelings. Self-compassion helps you become more comfortable with difficult emotions without judging yourself for having them. Instead of thinking, "I shouldn't feel this way," you can say, "I'm human, and it's okay to feel this way. God is with me in it." You'll experience true empathy when you extend that same understanding to yourself.

One of the most beautiful things about self-compassion is that it helps us to be present with our own pain, without running from it or pretending it isn't there. When we can sit with our own struggles and treat ourselves with kindness, we're better equipped to sit with others in theirs.

Think about it: when someone you care about is hurting, the last thing they need is to hear, "You should be over this by now," or "You're making a big deal out of nothing." Instead, what we need is someone who listens, someone who says, "I get it. I'm here for you." And that's what we can offer to others when we've learned to offer that same support to ourselves.

I've seen it firsthand in my own life. When I was feeling overwhelmed, I tried something simple. I took a deep breath and reminded myself, "I'm doing the best I can. It's okay to not be perfect. God loves me." It was easier to empathize with others when I was kind to myself. I wasn't so caught up in my own struggles that I couldn't hear someone else's.

God didn't design us to carry everything alone. We were made to love and support each other. But that starts with loving ourselves the way He loves us. If you've ever read the verse in Matthew 22:39, where Jesus says, *"Love your neighbor as yourself,"* you know that it starts with loving yourself. You can't give what you don't have. If you're not showing yourself kindness, how can you show it to others?

Self-compassion isn't about ignoring your struggles or pretending everything's okay when it's not. You need to acknowledge your pain. Understand that it's okay to feel weak while still allowing yourself the grace to heal at your own pace.

Remember, it's okay to not be okay. God's love for you is not dependent on your perfection. He loves you as you are. And as you learn to love yourself with that same unconditional love, you'll find it easier to love others in the same way.

Imagine a friend talking about their lack of success at work. When you listen with empathy, you are living out God's command to bear one another's burdens. When you don't judge their emotions, you let them know that you're there for them. This small act can encourage such people to share more and lessen feelings of isolation.

Stronger communities are built on understanding emotions as well. Jesus taught us to love our neighbors as ourselves. By noticing how others feel, you're more likely to act with kindness and thoughtfulness. A small gesture or a kind word can go a long way. These acts of compassion uplift others and bring God's light into their lives.

Congregations that are empathetic make for supportive communities that grow stronger. In the body of Christ, we are all connected and called to build each other up. Shared struggles become opportunities for everyone to strengthen themselves together through these connections, which become lifelines for anyone who feels isolated.

Recognizing someone's emotions and validating them deepens a relationship. In doing so, you are following the example of Christ. You're not just sharing their joys and pains; you're understanding their perspective. Shared experiences create truly genuine and open dialogue, which can transform your connections.

Expressing Empathy Through Actions

Simple acts of kindness, whether expressed through words or gestures, have an amazing impact on emotional challenges. Something as simple as smiling, holding a door open, or leaving an uplifting note can go a long way in helping someone who may be dealing with something difficult at that moment. Can you imagine the impact your small gestures could have on a person who is struggling to maintain their stability and hope? God's love is in these actions, and His compassion is there for those in need. As Jesus said, *"A new command I give you: Love one another. As I have loved you, so you must love one another. By this everyone will know that you are my disciples, if you love one another."* (John 13:34-35). During difficult times, your kindness can be a powerful way to share that love with others.

Taking kindness a step further involves listening with empathy and responding with understanding. When you show someone that their feelings count, you're telling them that you're there for them. For someone suffering from anxiety or sadness, it can be so comforting to know that they are understood and not forgotten about. Proverbs 17:17 says, *"A friend loves at all times."* Empathy is what you need to connect with a person and extend them the trust to go even deeper into healing.

When families, workplaces, or church communities are continually displaying empathy, they become a place for support and encouragement. Building strong networks of care can be as simple as checking in, offering help, or creating safe spaces to share. These are all simple one-on-one things you can do to ensure others feel supported. Knowing they have assistance in these networks helps people overcome challenges. It's an environment that, to an extent, nurtures people over time emotionally, spiritually, and with respect to their faith.

Sharing struggles with the people around you helps create stronger bonds, and it helps other people do the same, too. By being open about your struggles, you demonstrate to everyone that being vulnerable can help them heal, too.

This vulnerability mirrors the example of Christ, who shared in our suffering to bring us closer to God (Hebrews 4:15). Sharing helps others to experience connection and healing through mutual understanding and support. Personal stories create space by honoring everyone's challenges and by us being the body of Christ working together.

Break down walls of fear and inspire others through your story. As you share how God has worked in your life, you encourage people to trust Him with their own struggles. It creates a culture that's open and accepting to hearing someone's experience. Romans 12:15 reminds us to *"Rejoice with those who rejoice; mourn with those who mourn,"* and sharing your story sets the stage for these types of connections.

Summary and Reflections

It's important to remember that empathy is necessary for emotional healing. By listening and trying to see the world through another's eyes, we create connections to heal one (or many) of us. If you understand what it feels like to be anxious or depressed, someone else who is can feel like they're going to be understood when you reach out. Even little things, like kind words or gestures, can strengthen your relationships with others so that everyone can heal and grow.

Empathy reflects the heart of Christianity: compassion and love. It allows for safe spaces in which people can share their stories, be vulnerable, build trust, and deepen relationships. By doing so, you can deal with fear, worry, and mental health issues, and you can hold onto your spiritual faith while living in a practical way. Keep following this road of empathy and support. Inspired by Christ's love, you can help create a community of healing that shares hope and isn't a place where anyone has to struggle alone. When you help heal others, you're also helping yourself.

*"As I started opening up
and talking about my issues,
I felt strength, not vulnerability."*

~ Michael Phelps ~

Chapter 11: Faith's Role in Emotional Turmoil

It's your Christian faith that helps get you through those times when your emotions are in chaos. Your faith in God is a solid relationship you can rely on. It helps you feel a bit calmer and reassured when things feel a little shaky. Unlike emotions, which can be unpredictable and overwhelming, your faith provides a steady source of comfort and guidance. It means relying on God's strength and trusting that He is with you, especially during life's most difficult moments. Faith goes beyond hope—it's a deep belief in something greater that can completely transform how you see and face adversity.

Guidelines for Using Spiritual Support in Difficult Times

Set Boundaries for Spiritual Practices

When things get tough, it can feel like everyone is putting pressure on you to do it all perfectly, especially with your faith. I understand trying to balance everything and feeling like you're failing. One thing I've learned is that you're allowed to give yourself permission to be less than perfect with your spiritual practices when life is feeling heavy.

When tough times hit (and they will), setting boundaries on how you approach your faith can make a world of difference. For example, you might tell yourself that you "should" be reading your Bible for hours, praying daily, or experiencing joy and peace amidst all the chaos. So, when you strive to meet these expectations, you can quickly get burned out or feel like you're not enough.

Instead, try setting small, manageable goals for yourself. You might decide to spend just 10 minutes a day reading a verse or two or find a quiet spot for a few minutes of prayer without the pressure to "do it right." I've found that even on my toughest days, just a moment of stillness with God can make all the difference.

You need to create a space where you can breathe. Your faith doesn't need to be a source of stress—it should bring comfort, peace, and strength, even if you're just taking small steps. Allow yourself grace in the process. God isn't looking for perfection; He's looking for your heart. Setting these simple boundaries gives you room to rest and grow in ways that fit your situation. Your relationship with God doesn't have to be a checklist—it can be a loving, nurturing connection no matter what you're experiencing.

Have Patience with Your Own Healing

It's easy to wish you could snap your fingers and feel better when you're struggling, isn't it? I know how that feels because I have been there, wishing that the weight of it all would somehow just lift at an instant. The truth is, though, that healing—especially spiritual healing—takes time. You can't rush it. And that's okay.

There are moments when I would expect myself to bounce back quickly, and I would ask myself, "Why am I still struggling? Shouldn't I be feeling better already?" But I made my healing much harder because of those thoughts. I'd get mad at myself that I wasn't doing enough, wasn't praying enough, and wasn't trusting God enough. The pressure I was putting on myself only piled up, adding to my anxiety.

I learned something important over time. Healing won't happen overnight. It's a process. By trying to rush it, you deny yourself the peace and growth that can occur from waiting on God's time. Realizing that sometimes you don't have to have all the answers or be fully healed right away. God is calling you to trust Him and allow Him to heal you in His way.

It's not always easy, but giving yourself space and grace to heal is key. I've learned to stop judging myself for not 'feeling better' as quickly as I thought I should. I've learned to slow down and allow God to work in the quiet moments. That's where the growth happens—when you're not in a hurry, but you're trusting that God is working in the background, even if you can't see it just yet.

So, be patient with yourself. Don't rush the process. Remember, you don't need to meet a deadline for healing. Leave God to do His work and remember that you're exactly where you should be—growing, learning, and healing... in His time.

Allow Space for Grief and Emotions

It's easy to feel like you need to have it all together, especially as a Christian. Maybe you've told yourself that your faith should be enough to carry you through, so why are you still feeling so heavy? Let me tell you something I've learned: it's normal to grieve, cry, or feel overwhelmed when you're in an anxious state. Your emotions aren't something to shove aside, they're part of being human.

I remember a time when I was meeting up with some church members where I believed I needed to have it all together (whatever that means!). I didn't want anyone to see my sadness or fear because I was worried they would think my faith wasn't strong enough. The more I tried to hold it all in, though, the more it kept spilling out in ways I couldn't control. I was an absolute mess.

One kind lady took me aside and helped me through that moment. She told me that I shouldn't pretend to hold myself together; I just needed to let myself feel. I took my brokenness to God. I had no idea what to say, but I knew I had to be honest with Him and myself in that moment. He helped me move on from that experience. It's a day I'll never forget, though.

Grieving doesn't mean you're weak in your faith. It doesn't mean you're doing something wrong. Even Jesus wept when He felt the deep emotions of loss and love. If He, the Son of God, made space for grief, why wouldn't you? Your sadness, fear, or even anger can be a place where you meet God in a way that feels deeply personal. He's not expecting you to put on a show. He's ready to sit with you in your pain.

Let yourself feel what you're feeling. Give yourself permission to cry out to God, to journal your thoughts, or to simply sit quietly in His presence. Grief and pain aren't signs of a lack of faith—they're part of the process of healing and growing closer to Him. You don't have to have all the answers or fix everything. Just bring your heart, as it is, to God. He's big enough to handle it.

Creating Hope Through Faith

Your faith can offer something more than a quick fix or a temporary distraction. It gives you a deeper, lasting kind of hope that doesn't depend on your circumstances. Faith is about trusting that God is working alongside you, even when things seem to be falling apart.

Consider how Jesus approached challenging circumstances. He faced pain head-on and acknowledged its presence. In John 11, when Lazarus passed away, Jesus shared in the sorrow of Mary and Martha, even though He was aware that He would soon bring Lazarus back to life. That shows me it's okay to feel what you're feeling—to cry, grieve, and acknowledge unpleasant feelings. But it also reminds us that Jesus doesn't leave us there. He brings hope into those moments, showing that God's plan is bigger than our pain.

But sometimes, it's challenging to hold onto that hope. I've been there, struggling with my own doubts while clutching the thinnest of threads of faith. Grounding myself in simple truths seems to have helped me. I began to write down verses that resonated with me—verses like Isaiah 41:10: *"Do not fear, for I am with you; do not be dismayed, for I am your God."* On tough days, I'd pull those out and slowly read them, letting the words integrate into my mind. It was like a lifeline—a reminder that God is always with us even when the rest of our lives are shaky.

Something that's altered my outlook is gratitude. It feels impossibly hard to notice the positive things when you're overwhelmed. But starting small can help. Maybe it's the warmth of the sun on your face or a kind word from a friend. Writing down even one or two blessings each day has reminded me that God's goodness is still there, even in the middle of the mess.

Don't ignore what a difference it makes to listen to someone else's story. I remember a friend of mine saying how God helped her through a time of severe grief. It was exactly what I needed to hear at that moment: her openness about the struggle itself and the ways she turned to God.

If you're battling negative thoughts, faith can help there, too. When you catch yourself thinking, "I'm not enough," replace it with something true, like Ephesians 2:10: *"For we are God's handiwork, created in Christ Jesus to do good works."* Speak those words over yourself. Pray for them.

Even if it feels awkward at first, you'll be surprised how it starts to shift your mindset.

Through all of this, remember that God isn't asking you to handle everything perfectly. He's asking you to bring your struggles to Him. Exodus 14:14 says, *"The Lord will fight for you; you need only to be still."* That's not a promise of instant relief, but it is a call to put your burdens before his feet and believe he holds you.

Having faith doesn't take away the tough stuff, but it does provide you with something solid to hang on to. This is a hope that will not be destroyed by where we are or what we are going through. It's a hope that God is faithful, loving, and present, even on the hardest days.

Finding Solace in Prayer and Scripture

In times of anxiety, sadness, or simply the heaviness of the day-to-day, faith provides something very personal and sustaining. Prayer and reading scripture don't have to be just going through the motions. Devote your times of connection with God in your difficult moments to become meaningful and purposeful. These moments should serve as times of comfort, renewal, and trust, where you can present your burdens to God while finding strength through His presence.

For instance, prayer may be a lifesaver during an emotional struggle. It's not about the right words or some polished speech. That's just talking to God about your fears, your doubts, even your anger. Sometimes, I have cried out in prayer, "Lord, I don't know what to do. Help me."

And you know what? That's enough.

God doesn't need you to have it all together. He just wants you to come to Him. Zephaniah 3:17 *"The Lord your God is with you, the Mighty Warrior who saves. He will take great delight in you; in his love, he will no longer rebuke you but will rejoice over you with singing."* That peace is real—I've felt it, even in moments when nothing around me changed.

For me, gratitude has also been a game changer. It's easy to fall into a trap of focusing on what's wrong… and it can be really tempting to do that when things feel hard. However, taking the time to thank God for even the smallest blessings can change your whole outlook. Maybe it's a kind stranger or a quiet moment just when you needed it. Saying thank you in those moments doesn't erase what feels broken, but it does remind you that God's goodness is still present.

There's a story I love in Luke 17:11-19 where Jesus heals ten lepers, but only one comes back to thank Him. Jesus asks, *"Where are the other nine?"* That always hits me because it's so easy to forget gratitude when we're caught up in our struggles or even in our blessings. But pausing to acknowledge what God has done—even the little things—can open the door to deeper hope and trust.

Scripture is a comforting source that's always there for you. It's pretty amazing when you come across a verse that resonates with what you're dealing with. One of my favorites is Isaiah 43:2: *"When you pass through the waters, I will be with you; and when you pass through the rivers, they will not sweep over you."* That verse has carried me through some dark seasons, reminding me that God isn't just watching from a distance. He's right there in the middle of it, holding me steady.

One thing I've found helpful is to write verses down—on sticky notes, in a journal, or even as a lock screen on my phone. Seeing those words throughout the day brings moments of calm. Another verse that speaks to this is Matthew 11:29-30. *"Take my yoke upon you and learn from me, for I am gentle and humble in heart, and you will find rest for your souls. For my yoke is easy and my burden is light."* When you're hurting, you can feel like you're all alone. But verses like this remind you that you can rely on Jesus in those moments.

If you're like me, sometimes negative thoughts creep in, making it difficult to believe those promises. That's where affirmations rooted in scripture can be powerful. If you're feeling unworthy, you might tell yourself, *"I am fearfully and wonderfully made"* (Psalm 139:14). If you're doubting your strength, remind yourself, *"I can do all this through him who gives me strength."* (Philippians 4:13). Saying these truths out loud, even when you don't feel them, can start to shift your mindset.

Your faith gives you something steady to hold onto. God's promises are unchanging, and His love never fails. He's with you in every moment, offering peace, strength, and hope. You don't have to face your struggles alone—He's already gone before you, and He's walking beside you now.

Understanding the Transformative Power of Faith

Let's have a talk about how faith makes you see life differently. Faith isn't just for Sunday mornings. It's alive and active. It's how you face challenges, how you think, and even how you feel deep in your heart.

Faith Gives You a New Way of Seeing Things

Have you ever had a problem you thought you couldn't take on? How about that sinking feeling when you can't see a way out of a situation? Faith has an amazing way of changing your focus. Instead of obsessing over the problem, you start looking at God. After all, He is bigger than your problem.

Think about David facing Goliath. Everyone else saw a giant too big to fight, but David's faith let him see a giant that was too big for God to miss. Try using that kind of perspective on your problems. The switch in mindset will help you change how you see things.

Remind yourself that God is in control. He loves you dearly, and He has a purpose for you beyond your anxiety. Knowing this in your heart can make taking on your challenges feel easier when life gets messy. Romans 8:28 states, *"And we know that in all things God works for the good of those who love him, who have been called according to his purpose."* That doesn't mean everything will suddenly feel easy, but it does mean you can trust that God is working, even when you don't understand how.

Knowing Who You Are in Christ Changes the Game

A lot of anxiety comes from feeling like you're not enough: Like you're not smart enough, strong enough, or good enough. But you need to understand your worth isn't based on what you can or can't do. It's based on who God says you are.

You are His child, chosen and loved. Let that sink in for a minute. God doesn't look at you and see a list of mistakes or shortcomings. He sees someone worth sending His Son for.

Gideon's story in Judges 6 is a great example. He saw himself as the weakest in his family, but God called him a mighty warrior. Right now, you may be feeling weak, but you can do so much more than you know in God's hands.

Faith Requires Action

Faith isn't just about believing; it's about doing. That might sound intimidating, but stay with me. Think about Peter stepping out of the boat to walk on water. It wasn't the act of stepping that made the water hold him up; it was his trust in Jesus.

Faith is all about you taking those small steps, even when you're scared. It's praying when you don't want to, reading Scripture when all you want is to binge on Netflix, or reaching out to a friend when you're feeling the urge to isolate. If we choose to act in these small ways, guided by faith rather than fear, they accumulate and begin to reduce your anxiety.

Trusting God Instead of Being Controlled by Fear

Fear is sneaky, isn't it? It creeps in and takes over before you even realize it. But faith gives you something to hold onto when fear starts whispering in your ear.

Trusting God doesn't mean you won't feel afraid. It just means fear doesn't get the final say. When you focus on who God is—His goodness, His power, His promises—you start to loosen fear's grip.

One verse that helps me is Isaiah 26:3-4. *"You will keep in perfect peace those whose minds are steadfast because they trust in you. Trust in the Lord forever, for the Lord, the Lord himself, is the Rock eternal."*

Whenever fear tries to take over, remind yourself of this truth: God's got you.

Challenges Can Grow Your Faith

Nobody likes difficult times, but if we're honest, they're often the times when we grow the most. In those challenging times, you discover how to rely on God like never before.

James 1:2-4 says, *"Consider it pure joy, my brothers and sisters, whenever you face trials of many kinds, because you know that the testing of your faith produces perseverance. Let perseverance finish its work so that you may be mature and complete, not lacking anything."*

That doesn't mean you have to like the tough stuff, but it does mean God can use it for good.

The Holy Spirit Is Your Helper

As a Christian, one of the most comforting truths is that you don't have to face your anxiety without support. God's spirit, the Holy Spirit, is with you to guide you, comfort you, and give you strength when you're weak and afraid.

Have you ever been in a position where you didn't know what to say or do but still made it through? That is the work of the Holy Spirit. Jesus said in John 14:26 that the Holy Spirit would teach us and remind us of everything He said.

When you don't know what to pray about, Romans 8:26 says the Spirit intercedes for you. You don't have to have all the answers—just be willing to ask for help.

Experiencing God's Peace

Faith doesn't promise a life without problems, but it does promise peace in the middle of them. This is the kind of peace that doesn't make sense to the world.

2 Corinthians 13:11 is one of my go-to passages when I need to be reminded that peace isn't far away:

"Finally, brothers and sisters, rejoice! Strive for full restoration, encourage one another, be of one mind, live in peace. And the God of love and peace will be with you."

Peace isn't something you create on your own. It's a gift from God, and it's there for you when you take your worries to Him.

Faith Inspires Others

In the face of anxiety, choosing faith is not only for you; it is for everyone else as well. The individuals who are close to you will be able to witness it.

Try to picture Paul and Silas singing while they were in prison (Acts 16:25). Not only did they inspire one another with their faith, but it also influenced everyone who listened to them. The same is true for the strength that your religion possesses. In times of difficulty, when others see you putting your trust in God, it draws their attention to Him.

Faith and Worship Go Hand in Hand

Participating in worship is one of the most effective ways to strengthen your faith. The act of thanking God can take your focus away from the challenges you are facing and instead direct it toward Him, where it should be found.

When I was going through a particularly difficult season, I recall that I couldn't seem to get out of my thoughts. I switched on So Will I (100 Billion X), the song by Hillsong United, and it felt like a weight had been lifted off of my chest. This song brought to my mind the unwavering constancy of God, and I began to experience a renewed sense of hope.

Worship is a weapon against anxiety. Use it often.

Daily Practices That Build Faith

If you want faith to transform your life, it helps to build it into your daily routine. Here are a few ideas:

- Start your day with Scripture: Even just a verse or two can set the tone for your day.

- Pray throughout the day: It doesn't have to be fancy. Talk to God like you'd talk to a friend.

- Keep a gratitude journal: Write down three things you're thankful for each day. It shifts your focus from what's wrong to what's good.

- Find a community: Whether it's a small group, a trusted friend, or your church, having people to encourage you makes a big difference.

When everything is uncertain, the steadying aspect of your faith in God is reassuring. This doesn't mean you won't have challenging days, but it does mean you have something solid to hang onto, something bigger than what you're going through to lean on for peace and hope.

It's easy to forget that you don't need to carry life by yourself. Faith tells you to focus on God's strength, not your own. He sees your struggle; He sees your pain, and He walks you through it. As a result, when you feel lost or weighed down, take a moment, pause, pray, and remember who carries your future. Even when everything else seems to be changing, God's love for you is steadfast. Never let go of that truth. He's always right there with you.

> *"Anxiety is something
> that is part of me,
> but it's not who I am."*
>
> ~ Emma Stone ~

Chapter 12: Exploring Psychological and Spiritual Tools

When you're suffering from anxiety, it can feel like the two parts of you, the spiritual and emotional side, are separate or in conflict. What if there were a method to integrate them in a way that helped you heal and grow? In this chapter we'll see how psychological tools like Cognitive Behavioral Therapy (CBT) and professional therapy can complement your faith. We're looking to bring them together, not to create a divide. The goal is to have each one support the other for a more complete approach.

You don't have to choose between being a person of faith and taking care of your mental health. God doesn't want you to ignore your struggles or bottle up your emotions. He wants to help you work through them, using all the resources He's provided, including the knowledge we have about the mind. We'll look at some practical strategies you can use in your daily life and how they can complement your relationship with God to give you strength in unexpected ways.

This chapter will give you ideas on how to balance the psychological tools that help you feel better with the spiritual practices that deepen your connection with God. You'll see that your mental health care doesn't need to be a separate part of your life—it can be a space where your faith thrives alongside the help you're seeking.

Incorporating Therapy Alongside Christianity

Amazing healing and growth can occur by bringing together clinical mental health strategies with Christian practices. When you bring therapy and spirituality together, you can create a pathway that gives you both the practical tools and spiritual guidance you need to help you heal and thrive.

With professional therapy, you get strategies to manage your stress and anxiety. A competent therapist will help you to break yourself free from negative thought patterns and create healthier ones. Cognitive behavioral therapy (CBT) is a technique that can help you catch those automatic thoughts that tend to spiral out of control and help you change them to thoughts that are more positive.

Now couple these strategies with your faith, and they become even more powerful. Prayer, reflecting on scripture, and leaning on your church community are Christian practices that bring you comfort and a sense of purpose. Prayer and the practical work of therapy can go hand in hand. God sees you and is there to help you through your current struggles. You don't need to move through the darkness by yourself. His help, combined with the assistance of a therapist, is a powerful combination.

A competent therapist will provide you with the practical steps needed to move forward. Your faith provides the guardrails to keep you from falling, reminding you that you have God's steady hand in your life when it feels unsteady. Therapy and God working together, along with your will to heal yourself, make a strong team.

On occasion, people wonder if mixing faith and therapy will dilute one or the other. The truth is that they complement each other perfectly. Your faith gives you the motivation and deeper meaning that drives that growth. Therapy helps you understand your patterns and provides you tools for growth. For example, if you have social anxiety, therapy can include teaching you exposure techniques so you take steps toward facing your fears.

At the same time, your faith can remind you of scriptures like Deuteronomy 31:6. *"Be strong and courageous. Do not be afraid or terrified because of them, for the Lord your God goes with you; he will never leave you nor forsake you."* Together, these approaches give you both the practical steps and the spiritual courage to move forward.

If you're thinking about trying this blended approach, here are a few tips:

Be open with your therapist about your faith.

Let them know how important your beliefs are in your life and how you'd like to include them in your healing process.

Find someone who respects your faith.

Look for a therapist who values your Christian perspective and sees it as an asset, not something separate or unrelated to your mental health.

Create space for both therapy and spiritual practices.

Whether it's using therapeutic tools during your devotional time or journaling prayers and insights from therapy sessions, let the two approaches work together in your life.

It's also important to remember that you don't need to choose one over the other. Both psychology and spirituality are gifts from God. Therapy provides the skills you need to handle life's challenges, while faith keeps your heart connected to God's promises and love. Together, they give you a more complete way to face whatever comes your way.

This combination isn't a quick fix, and it doesn't make hard times magically disappear. But it does give you the strength to keep going, the wisdom to find new perspectives, and the peace that comes from knowing God is always with you. By bringing therapy and faith together, you're building a foundation for healing that's practical, spiritual, and deeply rooted in God's care for you.

Identifying the Right Therapist

Choosing the right therapist is an essential step when you're considering how to combine Christian faith with mental health strategies. It's important to find someone you feel will honor your Christian beliefs and acknowledge how influential they are in your life. Taking the time to find a therapist that respects your faith can make a world of difference.

Start with Someone Who Understands the Christian Faith

It's helpful to look for therapists who are open to incorporating Christian perspectives or those who specifically identify as Christian counselors. This might sound obvious, but it's essential. A therapist who understands the significance of faith will be more likely to make space for it and make you feel more comfortable talking about your spiritual life.A great place to begin is by checking online for licensed Christian therapists. There are lots of websites and organizations that feature professionals who incorporate faith into their work. One that covers the USA and Canada is *https://www.christiancounselordirectory.com/*.

Also, feel free to reach out to your church or community for some helpful suggestions.

Look for a Connection That Feels Right

Finding the right therapist is as much about connection and empathy as it is about qualifications. You want someone you feel comfortable with, someone who listens well and genuinely respects where you're coming from. Pay attention to how you are feeling during your first session or the initial consultation. Do they make you feel heard? Do you sense empathy and understanding?

A trustworthy therapist will not sideline your faith as something that can't be part of your healing process. They should be there to help you figure out how your beliefs can help your mental health and give you practical ways to handle whatever you are currently struggling with.

Share What Matters Most to You

Once you find someone that seems like a suitable fit, you need to have an honest conversation about what your expectations are. Tell the therapist how much your faith means to you and that you want it to be a part of your healing. Even if this feels like a vulnerable conversation, it's important work to lay the groundwork for your therapeutic work.

During your initial consultation, don't shy away from asking direct questions. How does the therapist approach faith in their sessions? Do they have experience working with Christians? Are they respectful of how important your Christian faith and practices are to you? Pay close attention to what they say. A genuine therapist who values your faith will understand and be open (and not try to minimize it or challenge you).

Keep the Conversation Going

Building a relationship where your Christian faith is honored means keeping communication open. Talk about your therapy goals and how you want faith to be involved. For example, maybe you'd like to include prayer in your sessions or use scripture as a source of encouragement when working through difficult emotions. Sharing these preferences early on helps create a partnership that feels genuine and encouraging.

When you work with your therapist, check in with yourself about how the process feels. Are you receiving spiritual understanding? Have you learned new ways to integrate faith and healing? And if something doesn't work, let it be known. Your voice matters, and therapy is a collaboration.

Be Patient and Stay Open

Finding the right therapist can take time. It's worth the effort to connect with someone who truly understands and respects your faith. Along the way, lean on your support system—your church, trusted friends, or online resources—to help guide you. The goal isn't just to find a therapist but to find someone who helps you grow both emotionally and spiritually.

Let Faith and Therapy Work Together

If you find that perfect match, you start to see how faith and therapy can really work together. Having faith gives you the peace and purpose to push through the dark times, but therapy gives you the practical tools to handle your anxiety or depression when times get tough. They make a foundation for healing that feels grounded and deeply rooted in God's care for you.

It won't be a fast or straightforward process, but it's a step forward you can take. When you find a therapist who respects your Christian beliefs and works with you in a way that honors them, you are creating space for true healing—healing that addresses both the heart and the spirit.

You should place your trust in God, walk with Him beside you, and approach the process step-by-step.

Moving Forward

Blending faith with mental health care isn't about following a strict formula. It's about creating a space where spiritual truths and psychological tools can work together. Both have value, and together, they can lead you toward healing that feels authentic and whole.

Keep showing up, keep seeking God, and keep trying new things. Some days will feel harder than others, but don't forget, God is with you, guiding you and offering strength for whatever comes next. Allow Him to guide you, and remember that healing is achievable, step by step.

Chapter 13: Holistic Lifestyle Improvements

Anxiety makes it a real challenge to have a balanced and peaceful life. However, if you step back and look at your day-to-day life as a whole, it can make a huge difference. Rather, the most help usually comes from a combination of small changes instead of desperately trying to fix just one part of your life. Staying active, moving your body in ways that feel good, connecting with others, and ensuring you get enough rest are all elements that can bring you long-lasting peace. They each support your body and mind and allow you to feel calmer and more grounded. It's not about being perfect; it's about making space for your own healing in your own way.

Incorporating Exercise into Your Mental Health Routine

We all know that exercise has been around forever as an amazing way to support both body and mind. But if you're a Christian wrestling with anxiety, fear, or even depression, regular movement can do wonders—right alongside prayer and your daily walk with God.

When you work out, your body lets loose some pretty awesome mood-lifting chemicals known as endorphins. Think of them as God-given little sparks of joy. They help balance out the stress hormones that ramp up your anxiety. Endorphins leave you feeling lighter and more at peace.

It's not just a quick fix, either. When you stick with a routine, exercise helps your brain become more flexible, making it easier to handle emotional ups and downs. As time goes on, you may notice that you feel less overwhelmed and more ready to tackle challenges, realizing that you've developed emotional strength.

But let's make this personal for a second—exercise isn't just about ticking something off a to-do list. It's a way to care for the body God gave you. Whether you're walking through your neighborhood, stretching on a yoga mat, or dancing around the living room to your favorite worship music, it's a chance to release pent-up stress and come back to a place of calm.

And here's something special: exercise can feel like a form of worship. By moving your body, you're honoring the gift of life God has entrusted to you. It's not just physical—it's spiritual too. Picture a brisk walk while you pray, or a run where you let your thoughts flow to God. Those moments can be deeply healing.

There's something wonderfully grounding about focusing on your body while you move. Whether it's the steady rhythm of your breath or the beat of your heart, it's a chance to quiet your mind and simply be present. It's a lot like prayer—a time to set everything else aside and find peace in the moment.

If the idea of adding exercise to your routine feels overwhelming, start small. Pick something you enjoy, even if it's just a few minutes here and there. Maybe try a group class or invite a friend along. Sharing the experience can make it more fun and encourage you when needed.

Don't think of exercise as separate from your spiritual life. Instead, let it complement your prayer time and Scripture study. It's one more way to care for yourself—mind, body, and soul—and keep anxiety in check. There are challenges in life, but God gave you tools to handle them. Exercise is one of those tools, and when coupled with faith, it can bring you peace and strength in ways you might not otherwise find.

Creating an Exercise Plan

You don't have to make it overly overwhelming or complicated when starting a workout routine that you can stick to. It's about identifying what is possible in your current situation and breaking things down into tiny, attainable steps. For a Christian seeking to take care of both the physical and mental body, this can be a way to glorify God. He has provided you with an amazing body, so it's important to take care of it.

First, look at your schedule honestly. Where are the small pockets of time that remain unoccupied? Perhaps the mornings are quieter, and you can fit in something before your day is in full swing, while the evenings are ideal for relaxing and walking after dinner. Choose a time and slot in your exercise in short bursts. It's not about fitting your life into a workout plan; it's about fitting movement into the life you already have.

The real secret? Pick the activities you actually like to do. What makes you smile? Do you enjoy dancing in your kitchen, riding a bike, playing basketball, or stretching on a yoga mat? Do what you love when you're low on motivation. Exercise doesn't have to be a chore; it can be a moment of joy in your day.

When you want to keep things interesting, mix it up. Tip: If one day you're walking, maybe the next day try a short workout video or do a sport. This variety stops you from getting bored and works out different parts of your body effectively. Having a few go-to options ensures you're always prepared to make time for exercise when an opportunity comes along in your day. The beauty of having an idea of your favorite options is that you can seamlessly switch activities if your plans change.

If you can, take it outside. Sometimes walking in the park, hiking a trail, or just walking through your neighborhood can do wonders. However, being in nature calms you and gets your body moving. Nature is perfect for disconnecting from ongoing stress and the chaos of the bustle of daily life. It is the best place to inhale deeply and maybe even do some box breathing. Nature is such a wonderful place for praying. You can gaze up at the sky and talk directly to God.

Start with small goals and keep them realistic. Enjoy a 20-minute walk a few times a week after dinner or do some gentle stretches before bedtime. The main thing is to begin somewhere. If every step counts and those small victories build confidence and momentum over time, then the idea is to keep winning.

Life will not always go as planned. It's okay if you miss a workout or need to change your schedule. Staying flexible and giving yourself grace will keep you far calmer.

Mindful Movement

Mindfulness goes perfectly hand in hand with movement. But they do not simply keep you active; they can also help soothe your anxiety and bring a little peace into your day. For Christians, this combination of mindfulness and movement cares for both your body and your soul. They are a great way to deepen your connection to God.

Let's explore how you can bring mindfulness into your physical activity in ways that are simple, grounding, and spiritually fulfilling.

One gentle example is yoga. If you've never done yoga before, don't be scared. Yoga uses gentle movement, stretching, and focused breathing through your diaphragm to calm your mind and strengthen your body. Yoga teaches you to maintain your focus on your breath and your attention in the present moment. This allows you to quiet racing thoughts that anxiety can bring on.

But yoga isn't just about calming your mind. It will help you to build flexibility, balance, and strength. Each stretch and movement is a chance to feel the body God gave you working as it should. While you're focusing on your breath, you might even find yourself in quiet prayer, thanking Him for the gift of movement and calmness. There are some fabulous YouTube videos covering relaxation yoga.

Yoga Nidra is another form that is also worth looking at. This meditative form of yoga aims to guide you into the transitional state between wakefulness and sleep. It's very relaxing and helpful if you are struggling to sleep through the night.

And if yoga isn't your thing, there are other options. Mindful movement can take many forms. One of my favorites is walking. It's a very easy way of practicing mindfulness. If you find yourself rushing from point A to point B, consciously slow down your pace. Pay attention during your walk to your surroundings, the air, and the pavement. Take it one step and one breath at a time and let go of some of that stress every time your foot touches the ground.

Another gentle option to consider is Tai Chi. Tai Chi is a gentle, flowing practice that combines slow, intentional movements with focused breathing. It's been used in Asia for centuries for mindfulness, making it a wonderful way to calm an anxious mind. Tai Chi is simple once you learn the basics (hello, YouTube University!). You don't need special equipment or a specific location to practice it, just a bit of space and a willingness to slow down. As a Christian, you can bring your faith into the practice by using this quiet time to reflect on God's presence in your life. Tai Chi is great for letting go of tension and feeling more grounded, all while keeping your focus on the One who offers rest for your soul.

Focused breathing is another way to add mindfulness to your activities, whether it's during exercise or when meditating. Your brain sends a message to your nervous system to relax when you intentionally slow down and pay attention to your breath. It's simple—just take a deep breath in through your nose for a count of four, hold it for a count of four, and then gently let it out through your mouth. You can also use focused breathing when doing activities such as running, cycling, or swimming. In fact, any exercise that has a consistent rhythm is perfect for focused breathing. Every time you find your mind wandering, concentrate on syncing your breath back in time with your movement.

If you'd like, you could also mix walking meditation with prayer for a more intense connection with God. You could start by meditating on a verse that speaks to you, like Psalm 55:22. *"Cast your cares on the Lord and he will sustain you; he will never let the righteous be shaken."* Repeat this verse to yourself as you walk, allowing it to calm you down.

If structured activities feel too rigid, don't overthink it. Mindful movement is very simple. Try turning on some worship music and dancing in your living room, stretching while you listen to a sermon, or even tending to your garden while thanking God for His creation. The key is to stay present and to invite God into your heart and mind. Start in the present moment and don't put pressure on yourself to get it perfect.

To bring mindfulness into physical activities and maximize these dual benefits, consider these guidelines:

1. **Start Simple:** Begin by incorporating brief moments of mindfulness into your regular routine. As you start any exercise, whether yoga, running, or walking, take a few minutes to center yourself. Set an intention to remain present and aware throughout your practice.

2. **Prioritize Consistency:** Designate specific times for your mindful activities, treating them as indispensable appointments with yourself. Consistency cultivates habit formation and ensures that the benefits permeate all areas of life.

3. **Reflect Regularly:** After each session, spend a few moments reflecting on the experience. Journaling about the thoughts, feelings, and insights that arose during the activity can deepen your self-awareness and reinforce the benefits.

4. **Adapt Practices:** Tailor mindfulness techniques to suit your preferences and lifestyle. Flexibility in your approach ensures sustainability and prevents the feeling of mindfulness becoming another task to complete.

5. **Engage in Mindful Networks:** Consider joining groups or classes focused on mindful physical activities, like yoga studios or walking clubs. Sharing experiences and learning from others can enhance commitment and enjoyment.

Community Engagement

Joining an exercise group is perfect if you are the kind of person who feels more motivated when you're around others. For Christians, it's an opportunity to care for your body while connecting with others in a way that reflects God's design for community. Besides, working out with other people can be fun. It helps you direct your attention toward others and get you out of your anxious mindset.

When you join a group like this, you're putting yourself into a supportive environment where people will hold you accountable if that's what you need. Knowing that someone is expecting you to show up makes it a little harder to skip your exercise session, even on those tough days. Team sports are also excellent for this added incentive. And let's be honest—those tough days come for all of us. Having others there with you is a blessing from God.

The connections you build in these groups can be really helpful when healing from anxiety. Sure, you're working out together, but it's also about the conversations you'll have and the friendships you'll create. For those of us who've felt the weight of anxiety or isolation, this is a gift. God often uses other people to lighten your load, and you never know what new relationships you'll form by expanding your network of acquaintances.

One of the best parts of an exercise group is celebrating each other's progress. Whether it's reaching your first or next fitness milestone or simply showing up on a day when it would've been easier to stay home, this kind of group could be just what you need. You'll find people who will listen, support, and remind you of your progress.

When you find the right group (just like finding the right therapist if you need one), you'll notice a pattern of support and inspiration. Someone you share a sport with might inspire you to push a little harder, while your own progress might motivate someone else to keep going. Over time, you'll find that the consistency and discipline you've been working toward feel a little easier, thanks to your new fitness friends.

And don't worry about not "being fit enough" to join. Exercise groups are usually made up of people at all different levels. You'll see beginners, seasoned athletes, and everyone in between. That mix creates an environment where you can learn from others, try new things, and feel comfortable being at your own level. There's no pressure to do anything but grow and improve alongside each other. Don't forget, there's always a beginner group for most sports or exercise classes.

When you weave your faith into these experiences, something special happens. Praying before or after a workout or encouraging each other with faith-filled words can add a sense of purpose to what you're doing. That connection between the physical and spiritual makes the time you spend with the group even more meaningful.

If you're thinking about joining an exercise group, take some time to find one that feels right for you. It should be a place where you feel welcomed and comfortable—a space that reflects your values and encourages your growth. Some local churches will also offer a variety of groups. Don't be scared to try a couple of classes or sports until you find something that clicks. When you do, it will no longer feel like 'one more thing to do.' Instead you'll become part of a community you are pleased to be a part of.

The friendships you build in these settings can carry on long after you've stopped working out together. Your new friends could become a part of the foundation of a healthy and joyful life. And the more you grow physically, emotionally, and spiritually, the better prepared you will be to deal with what life throws at you.

If you've been doubtful, let this be that encouragement you've been waiting for to take the next step. Whether it's your first time lacing up your sneakers or you're looking for a fresh start, there's a group out there so excited to invite you in with open arms. And who knows? You might be surprised to discover that the time you spend there could become one of the most relaxing parts of your week.

Developing Healthy Sleep Habits

When you're living with anxiety, sleep can feel elusive. Lying awake with a racing mind is the most common cause of insomnia. It's tough to stop yourself from replaying the day or worrying about tomorrow. Even when anxiety tries to interfere, you can build habits that promote better sleep if you make a few changes and tweaks.

Sleep is one of God's gifts, a way for our bodies and minds to restore. Consider it a time to refill your cup so you can wake up refreshed and ready to serve Him again. I want to help you learn some things you can do to improve your sleep habits (something that is often closely linked with anxiety) in a more actionable way.

Create a Calming Bedtime Routine

Your mind needs time to shift from "go mode" to "slow mode." Building a peaceful pre-bedtime ritual can signal to your brain that it's time to wind down.

- Set a consistent bedtime: Go to bed and wake up at the same time daily. This rhythm helps your body know when it's time to sleep and when it's time to wake. Anxiety thrives on unpredictability, so being strict with your schedule will help.

- A sleep timetable will help. Obviously, if you are a shift worker or have varying work times, this is difficult to achieve. If that's the case, keep reading for some tips that will help you.

- Spend time with God: Before you settle into bed, take some time for prayer or reading the Scripture from a paper Bible. No devices allowed. Meditating on God's Word can help you to redirect anxious thoughts. Psalm 4:8 says, *"In peace I will lie down and sleep, for you alone, Lord, make me dwell in safety."* This is the perfect verse for anxious hearts before bedtime.

- Avoid screens: Phones, tablets, and TVs emit blue light that can trick your brain into thinking it's daytime. And endless scrolling is anxiety-inducing. If you've been on your phone during the evening, try swapping your screen time for something relaxing, like a candlelit bath or soft worship music.

You should treat your bedroom as your sanctuary. It should be peaceful and have very few distractions. Small adjustments can make a big difference.

- Keep your room cool and dark: A slightly cooler room temperature helps your body stay comfortable, so use a fan or air conditioner to snuggle under a blanket. Also, darkness signals to your brain to produce melatonin, the hormone that makes you sleepy. A sleep mask can help a lot. While they require a few nights to adjust to, their benefits are well worth the time. I sometimes only wear mine in the morning to block out the light before getting out of bed.

- Declutter your space: A tidy room can help quiet your mind. Too much clutter can subconsciously create a sense of chaos. It might be time to declutter your bedroom Marie Kondo style!

- Invest in a comfy mattress and pillows: If your bed isn't comfortable, your sleep quality will suffer. Think of this as an investment in your health and well-being. You should change your mattress every ten years, or even more frequently if possible.

- Use soothing scents: Lavender and chamomile are known for their calming properties. A diffuser with essential oils or a linen spray can help you relax at bedtime.

What You Eat Impacts How You Sleep

Your diet plays a huge role in how you sleep, so what you eat should be something you focus on. One approach that's helped many people, including me, is eating a low-carb or no-carb diet. Once your body adjusts, this way of eating can lead to some of the most restful sleep you've ever had. Keeping your blood sugar levels stabilized will mean you wake up less during the night, giving you a deeper, more restorative sleep.

Some other food-related tips:

- Avoid caffeine after midday: Even if you don't feel jittery, coffee can stay in your system for hours and disrupt your ability to fall asleep.

- Watch your sugar intake: Eating high-sugar snacks before bed will spike your energy. This can cause a 'sugar crash,' which may be waking you up in the middle of the night.

- Enjoy herbal teas: Have a warm cup of chamomile or peppermint tea in the evening to help calm your mind and get you ready for bed.

Prepare for Anxiety's Nighttime Tricks

An anxious mind loves to get loud at night. It's when the world quiets down that your thoughts seem to shout the loudest. Preparing well for this time of day can help you feel more in control.

- **Journal your thoughts:** Write down anything that is on your mind for at least five to ten minutes before bed. Putting pen to paper will help offload your worries from the day.

- **Practice deep breathing:** Concentrated breathing will bring your nervous system to a calm state and back to being present. This is the perfect time to use the box breathing technique.

- **Speak truth over fear:** Remind yourself of God's faithfulness. Have a verse ready to repeat when anxiety strikes, like 2 Timothy 1:7: *"For the Spirit God gave us does not make us timid, but gives us power, love and self-discipline."*

Limit Stimulants and Disruptions

Sometimes, the things we allow into our days—and nights—can quietly disrupt our sleep. Being mindful of these unhelpful influences can help you sleep a lot better.

- **Limit news and heavy conversations at night:** If the news or certain discussions raise your anxiety, save them for earlier in the day. Also, you can stop watching the news or at least reduce your consumption of it.

- **Skip naps or keep them short:** Long naps can throw off your body's natural rhythm. If you need a rest, aim for 20 or 30 minutes earlier in the afternoon.

- **Avoid eating large meals late:** A heavy dinner may make you have a difficult time falling asleep comfortably.

Give Yourself Grace

Building healthy sleep habits takes time. Some nights will still be hard, and that's okay. When those nights come, remind yourself that God's strength is made perfect in weakness (2 Corinthians 12:9). You don't have to get everything perfect; just keep working at making changes until your sleep improves. One trick I learned from an ex-paramedic who struggled with sleep was to say, 'Rest is as good as sleep,' over and over when falling asleep is a struggle.

Spending Time with Friends

God designed us for connection. From the very beginning, He made it clear that relationships are a core part of who we are. Proverbs 27:17 says, *"As iron sharpens iron, so one person sharpens another."* This isn't just about growth or accountability—it's also about joy. Spending time with friends lifts us up, brings laughter into our lives, and helps ease the weight of stress and anxiety.

But here's a question to pause and consider: When was the last time you really had fun? Not just a smile here or there, but real, soul-deep joy. The kind that makes you laugh until your stomach hurts or forget for a moment all the things weighing on your heart.

Right through my own period of anxiety, the idea of fun was my nemesis. And that question, 'When was the last time you really had fun?' would make me cry. I didn't even know how to have fun at the time.

Now, at the age of 50, I have obtained my motorcycle license. Riding is fun and puts a huge smile on my face. I realized that I hadn't allowed myself the joy of this since I wanted to get my license in my early 20s.

The Gift of Laughter and Joy

Laughter is a gift from God. It's a reminder of His goodness and the beauty in life, even when things feel heavy. Proverbs 15:13 tells us that *"a happy heart makes the face cheerful, but heartache crushes the spirit."* Fun and joy don't just make life feel lighter; they're part of what keeps us emotionally and spiritually healthy.

It's easy to get caught up in the seriousness of life. Work deadlines, family responsibilities, financial stress, and even the ongoing battle with anxiety can push simple joys to the back burner. But those carefree moments with friends aren't just indulgent—they're necessary. They remind us that God's blessings can be found in even the smallest giggles and shared moments.

Reflecting on Your Last Moment of Fun

Think back: when was the last time you let yourself fully enjoy time with a friend? Maybe it was a long chat over coffee, a game night full of laughter, or a spontaneous outing that left you smiling for days. Or maybe it's been so long that you're struggling to remember. If that's the case, maybe now is the time to make a change. Life's demands can crowd out these moments if we're not careful.

Reconnecting Through Intentional Friendship

The good news is that it's never too late to make time for fun and friendship again. It doesn't have to be complicated or perfect—what matters is showing up and being present. Here are a few simple ways to reconnect:

- **Plan a Low-Key Get-Together:** Host a game night, invite a friend for coffee, or go for a casual walk. Keep it simple so it feels manageable.

- **Reach Out:** Think of one friend you haven't spoken to in a while and send them a text or call. A quick message can go a long way in rekindling a connection.

- **Share a Laugh:** Send a funny meme, video, or memory to a friend. Laughter is often the first step to reconnecting.

- Be Open to Spontaneity: Say yes to an invite, even if it's last minute or outside your comfort zone. Sometimes the best memories are the ones we don't plan.

Finding Joy in Fellowship

God designed us for connection. Ecclesiastes 4:9-10 says, *"Two are better than one, because they have a good return for their labor: If either of them falls down, one can help the other up. But pity anyone who falls and has no one to help them up."* Friendships are all about joy. They bring laughter into our lives, ease the weight of stress and anxiety, and in general, lift us up. Spending time with friends isn't just fun—it's a way to nurture your soul and glorify God through fellowship.

So, who can you reach out to this week? Maybe it's someone you've been meaning to call or a friend you miss seeing. Take that step, no matter how small. Allow yourself to rediscover the joy of friendship, and don't forget to thank God for the blessing of people who bring light and laughter into your life.

Laughter Therapy: A Gift from God

Proverbs 17:22 tells us, *"A cheerful heart is good medicine, but a crushed spirit dries up the bones."* Fun and joy don't just make life feel lighter; they're part of what keeps us emotionally and spiritually healthy.

Laughter therapy is one of the most fun ways to ease anxiety. When something silly makes you laugh so hard your stomach hurts, you forget your worries in the moment. That's the beauty of laughter. It resets the neural pathways in your brain and gives your heart a little room to breathe.

Here are a few ways you can give it a try:

- Watch a funny movie
- Listen to audio of kids giggling
- Dust off your old favorite childhood cartoons that made you laugh
- Try a laughter yoga video (sometimes just fake laughing turns into the real thing)

- Read a hilarious book or collection of funny short stories
- Play charades or Pictionary
- Scroll through a funny social media account dedicated to clean humor
- Watch a stand-up comedy special or clean comedy skits on YouTube
- Laugh at your own mistakes
- Watch blooper reels
- Watch funny animal videos (cat zoomies!)

These can all help you shake off a stressful day. A cheerful heart truly is the best medicine.

Reflections

If you're already living with anxiety, making changes to your lifestyle can seem like a lot to take on. The good news is all the small steps you do take do add up, and God is with you in every one of those small steps. Regardless of whether your focus is on sleep, food that works with you, or movement that brings you joy, these are things that speak to how we care for the temple that God has given to us. Perfection and performance don't have anything to do with it. Living in a way that respects both your physical and spiritual well-being is honoring yourself and God.

As you start to integrate these habits, make sure to do so with grace. Certain days will be easier than others. Show up with intention and lean on God during the process. When you begin to take care of yourself—body, mind, and soul—you are making room for His peace to reside and calm the storm of anxiety. Know that He is pleased with your efforts and is walking with you toward a life that's more balanced and calmer.

Chapter 14: Vulnerability

When you're feeling anxious, it can feel like no one understands what you're experiencing. However, there's something magical that happens when you open up and let yourself be vulnerable to others. Even if that idea is absolutely terrifying to you, sharing your worries can help you feel less isolated.

When you're open about what you're facing—whether it's with a trusted friend, a family member, or someone in your church community—you're creating space for connection. Vulnerability brings other people into your world in a way that builds empathy and understanding. Suddenly, it's not just you that's carrying the weight on your own. There's someone else standing beside you, ready to listen and support you.

In these moments of honesty, your willingness to be open and share your struggles lightens your emotional load. It also encourages those around you to share their experiences with anxiety, too. It's a ripple effect; one person's bravery inspires another's.

In a world that constantly screams at us to 'have it all together,' being vulnerable and sharing that we are not okay is a rebellious act.

Faith plays such a big role here, too. When you share your struggles with those who share your belief in God, it creates an opportunity to come together in His eyes. Those moments of shared faith can be deeply comforting. They remind you that not only are others walking alongside you, but God is right there with you, offering strength and peace.

Being vulnerable doesn't mean you have to share every detail of your life with everyone. You need to regulate how much you share so you feel safe. Taking that first step to share your struggles might feel uncomfortable, but it's often the beginning of real healing.

Vulnerability in the Context of Faith

Vulnerability is about sharing the deepest parts of yourself—your fears, doubts, and even your pain—and trusting God with every bit of it. It's more than being honest about how you feel, though that's part of it. It's about coming before Him as you are, without any filters or pretenses, and letting Him meet you there. Part of Psalm 62:8 says, *"Pour out your heart before Him,"* and that simple image holds so much meaning.

God doesn't ask for the polished, picture-perfect version of you. He wants the real you—the one who might feel unsure, scared, or even broken. That's where the most genuine connection begins.

Being vulnerable is risky, especially when you're emotionally fragile. We're told to bottle up our feelings, to be strong, to never let anyone see when we're struggling. With God, vulnerability isn't a sign of weakness, though. In fact, it's one of the boldest things you can do. Saying to God, "I can't do this alone; I need You," shows incredible strength. You're admitting that you don't have the power to hold everything together, but you do have the power to rely on Him.

Opening yourself up to God also means letting go of control, which can be hard. There's a natural tendency to hold onto certain parts of your life, thinking you can manage them better on your own or shield yourself from pain. But when you're willing to loosen that grip and trust Him, you give Him room to work in ways you might not expect.

Surrendering doesn't mean giving up—it means choosing to believe that God's plans are bigger and better than anything you could imagine. That kind of trust builds a deeper relationship with Him, one rooted in love and faith.

Being vulnerable with God is a reminder that you don't have to have all the answers. He's not asking for perfection or strength all the time. He wants the real you—the unguarded you. When you come to Him with your heart in your hand, He will gift you with peace and strength. So, take a step of faith. Pour out your heart, let Him carry your burdens, and trust that He will be there with love and grace.

Jesus as the Ultimate Example of Vulnerability

When you think of Jesus, you may think of His miracles, His boldness, or His unending love for others. But have you ever stopped to consider how vulnerable He was? Jesus didn't hide His humanity, and that's one of the most beautiful and relatable things about Him. He wasn't afraid to show pain or express deep emotions. Instead, He embraced them fully, giving us a clear picture of what it looks like to trust God while being honest about the challenging stuff.

Take the Garden of Gethsemane. Jesus knew what was coming—the betrayal, the physical torment, the unbearable weight of the world's sin—and He didn't bottle up His feelings or try to face it alone. He prayed, *"My soul is overwhelmed with sorrow to the point of death"* (Matthew 26:38). That's raw honesty. He didn't sugarcoat His emotions or try to present a "strong front." Instead, He poured out His heart to God, laying bare all the anguish He was carrying. Even as He wrestled with what was ahead, He surrendered, saying, *"Not as I will, but as you will"* (Matthew 26:39). That moment is such a powerful reminder of what trust in God looks like—even when it's hard, even when it hurts.

Jesus didn't face that moment completely alone. He brought Peter, James, and John with Him, asking them to stay close and pray. He let them see His sorrow and asked for their support, showing us how important it is to lean on others during difficult times. Vulnerability isn't about being weak; it's about being real—real with God and real with the people you trust.

Then there's the moment at Lazarus's tomb, where we find the shortest verse in the Bible: *"Jesus wept"* (John 11:35). Think about that. Even though Jesus knew He was about to raise Lazarus from the dead, He didn't skip over the grief. He allowed himself to feel the weight of the loss, and he cried openly. That verse alone can remind us that emotions aren't something to be hidden or pushed away. If Jesus, the Son of God, wept in public, you can too.

Jesus shows you through His vulnerability that you don't fail in faith by being open about your pain, fear, or sorrow. It means you're human. Being real with God in those moments brings you closer to Him. When you're overwhelmed, or you're hurting, don't hesitate to cry out to Him.

He knows every tear, every prayer, and every unspoken feeling, and He's right there, holding you through it.

The Connection Between Vulnerability and Anxiety

As a human, your base instinct is to hide anxiety when it creeps into your life. You might put on a smile, say you're fine, and try to shove those feelings into a corner where you hope they'll stay quiet. The reality is, those feelings don't go away; they just get bigger until you heal them. The walls you think are protecting you often end up boxing you in, making the weight of your anxiety feel even heavier. Pretending everything is okay doesn't make the pain disappear; it just cuts you off from the people who care about you and want to help.

Opening up about anxiety can feel terrifying. Saying out loud that you're struggling might make you feel exposed. None of us like revealing something we'd rather keep hidden. What if someone doesn't understand? What if they judge you? These worries are real, but keeping it all bottled up isn't the answer. Anxiety loves secrecy—it grows stronger in the dark. But when you bring those feelings into the light, you start to break its grip.

Being vulnerable—whether with a friend, a family member, or God—can feel like exhaling after holding your breath for too long. It's freeing. And when you pour out your heart to God, something amazing happens. Psalm 62:8 says, *"Trust in him at all times, you people; pour out your hearts to him, for God is our refuge."* God doesn't need you to come to Him with perfect words or a polished version of yourself. He just wants the real you. The you who's hurting, scared, and unsure. When you let Him into those difficult places, you'll find comfort in knowing He's there with you, carrying what feels too heavy to bear alone.

It doesn't mean that just because you share your struggles, they'll be gone. It does lighten the burden, though. But when you let people see who you really are, you give them the opportunity to connect with you in a deeper way. There are others who are able to walk alongside you when you are vulnerable.

So take that first step, even if it's just a small one. Open up to someone you trust. Pour out your heart in prayer, even if it feels messy. You don't have to carry the weight of anxiety alone. When you let others in, you might find that the peace you've been longing for was closer than you thought.

Practical Ways to Embrace Vulnerability

Let's be real. Being vulnerable isn't something that comes easily to most of us. It feels safer to keep things to yourself and put on a brave face for the outside world. After all, digging too deep into the harder stuff isn't pleasant. Maybe you think if you ignore those difficult emotions, they'll fade away. But you and I both know that doesn't happen. The more you hold things in, the more isolated you feel, and eventually, the weight becomes too much.

The first step is being honest about where you're holding back. Is it in your prayers, where you only say what feels "acceptable" instead of pouring out what's really on your heart? Perhaps you hide your struggles in your relationships because you fear judgment. Maybe it's with your partner, or maybe it's with yourself. Do you avoid naming what's really going on because it feels too big to face? That said, it's not easy to take an honest look at those areas, but if you don't, you'll never be able to break free from that cycle. If you're feeling that way, go back to Chapter 5, which covered processing emotions.

When it comes to opening up to God, remember this: He already knows every detail of what you're carrying. You don't have to filter your words or put on a spiritual mask. Psalm 34:18 says, *"The Lord is near to the brokenhearted and saves the crushed in spirit."* God isn't asking for polished prayers—He wants your real, raw, unedited self. If it helps, try writing down your prayers or just sitting quietly with Him, saying whatever comes to mind. Even if all you can manage is, "God, I'm struggling," that's enough.

Being vulnerable with others can feel even scarier, but you don't have to share everything all at once. Start small. Talk to someone you trust—your partner, a friend, a family member, or maybe someone from your church—and share one thing you're dealing with. You'll often find that when you're honest, it encourages others to be honest too. Vulnerability creates connection, and the right people will meet you with understanding, not judgment.

Don't forget to be honest with yourself. When anxiety or pain rears its ugly head, it's tempting to shove it aside and pretend you're fine. But it's okay to admit when things are hard. Give yourself the grace to feel what you're feeling. Tell yourself, "This is tough, but I don't have to have it all together right now." God isn't asking for perfection, and you shouldn't ask it of yourself either.

Choosing vulnerability isn't about exposing your weaknesses—it's about opening the door to deeper relationships and real peace. When you stop pretending and start being real—with God, with others, and with yourself—you'll find that you're never as alone as you thought. There's strength in letting go of the mask and allowing yourself to be known, just as you are.

How to Overcome Barriers to Vulnerability

Being vulnerable is uncomfortable. You might wonder if people will see your struggles and think less of you or, worse, step back entirely. And maybe you've told yourself that looking strong is what you're supposed to do, even when you feel like you're barely holding it together. That fear of being judged or misunderstood can keep you silent, but it doesn't have to.

Here's something to hold on to: vulnerability isn't weakness. The Bible flips that idea on its head. In 2 Corinthians 12:9, Paul says, *"My grace is sufficient for you, for my power is made perfect in weakness."* When you stop trying to carry everything on your own, you create space for God to step in and do what only He can. Those walls you've built to protect yourself might feel safe, but they can also block you from experiencing God's love and the kind of connection He designed you for.

It's normal to feel hesitant—it's hard to open up when fear of rejection looms large. But the truth is, God's love doesn't waver, as shown in Joshua 1:9. *"Have I not commanded you? Be strong and courageous. Do not be afraid; do not be discouraged, for the Lord your God will be with you wherever you go."* When you're scared to let people see the real you, remind yourself that God already does. He sees it all and loves you anyway.

That first step doesn't need to be dramatic. Start small. Maybe it's a quiet prayer like, 'I can't open up about my anxiety, so I need your help,

God.' Or it may be asking a friend you trust to reach out and say, 'Hey, there's something I've been holding onto, and I need to talk about it.' You don't have to share everything at once; just open up a little and ask for more help the next time you meet up. Vulnerability is a process, and it's okay to take it one step at a time.

Here's the thing—when you let people in, the ones who truly care won't turn away. They'll walk with you through it. Even if some don't, God never will. He's with you in every moment of doubt, every tear, and every hesitant step forward. Trust that He's working in and through your honesty, breaking down those walls bit by bit. You don't have to do this perfectly—just start. God's grace will carry you the rest of the way.

The Role of Vulnerability in Relationships

Even our most cherished relationships aren't always easy, are they? That can include your relationship with God. You might love someone deeply but still hold back pieces of yourself. Maybe you don't want to weigh them down, or you're afraid they won't know what to do with your struggles. But here's the thing: when you let yourself be honest with the people who truly care about you, you create a deeper connection. Real trust starts to grow in those messy, unfiltered moments.

Think about the people closest to you. It could be your spouse, your best friend, or your family. When you've shared something personal, maybe even something hard, hasn't that brought you closer? Vulnerability is like saying, "This is me, the real me, and I trust you enough to let you see it." It doesn't weaken a relationship; it makes it stronger. And when someone else trusts you with their heart, it's humbling, isn't it? You feel honored to hold that space for them.

God gives us a beautiful reminder of this in Galatians 6:2: *"Carry each other's burdens."* That's His design for our relationships. We're not meant to walk through life on our own. When you share what's on your heart, you allow others to step up and support you. And when someone opens up to you, you're doing the same for them. In the willingness to be there for one another, the beauty of God's love shows up.

Being vulnerable can feel very risky, even if you're disclosing something to your partner. Never rule out the possibility that they won't respond as expected. What if they don't get it? That's where you need to trust in God to guide the moment and use it for good, even if it doesn't go perfectly. Being vulnerable means being brave enough to open up to others when you're not sure you should.

Healing Through Vulnerability

There's something about keeping your struggles hidden that seems to make them louder, isn't there? When pain, shame, or anxiety stays locked inside, it feels like it starts whispering lies—convincing you that you're all alone or too far gone for anyone to understand. But here's the thing: those struggles lose their power when you bring them into the light. Vulnerability is the first step toward breaking free from the grip of fear.

1 John 1:7 puts it beautifully: *"But if we walk in the light, as he is in the light, we have fellowship with one another, and the blood of Jesus, his Son, purifies us from all sin."* Walking in the light, in the biblical sense, is about choosing openness instead of isolation. It's letting God and the people you trust see the weight you've been carrying—whether it's fear, doubt, or that voice in your head telling you you're not enough. That's where healing begins.

Think back to a time when you finally shared something heavy you'd been holding in. Maybe you opened up to a friend about a burden you've been carrying for years, and they helped you to heal. Did you feel like a painful emotion was released? When you step into vulnerability, it makes space for connection. God's grace is big enough to meet you right there, even in the difficult parts of your life.

Of course, the enemy loves to keep you stuck in silence. He'll plant thoughts like, "No one will get it," or, "If they knew this about you, they'd never look at you the same." But those are just lies meant to hold you back. Vulnerability shuts down those lies by stepping into God's truth: you are fully loved, even in your weakest, most uncertain moments.

Healing is a process. You may have to make the choice to be vulnerable over and over again. When you let go of the weight you've been carrying, you'll discover something amazing. That being fully known by God and the people He placed in your life brings a peace that silence never could.

God's Grace in Our Vulnerability

You don't have to hide your imperfections or weaknesses. It's easy to feel that you have to keep it all together. You may want to prove to the world that you are strong, capable, and unshakeable. But that's not what God asks of you. His love isn't something you earn by having it all figured out, and His grace doesn't wait for you to get your act together. It meets you right where you are—mess, struggles, and all.

It brings to mind that powerful quote from Isaiah 40:29-31: *"He gives strength to the weary and increases the power of the weak. Even youths grow tired and weary, and young men stumble and fall; but those who hope in the Lord will renew their strength. They will soar on wings like eagles; they will run and not grow weary; they will walk and not be faint."* Think about that for a second. The very places you might see as weak or flawed are the ones where God's strength shines the most. That's hard to wrap your head around sometimes, isn't it? But it's true. God's power doesn't show up in your perfection. It shows up when you lean on Him, when you say, "God, I need You."

Letting yourself be vulnerable doesn't mean you're failing. It doesn't mean you're broken beyond repair. It means you're human, and it's in that honesty that God meets you with His strength. When you stop pretending you've got it all under control, you make space for God to work in ways you couldn't even imagine. And you'll find that His grace isn't just enough—it's more than enough.

It's okay to admit you're in a tough spot right now. Maybe it feels like you're running out of strength because you've been carrying the weight of something for a long time. I've been there. God sees you, and He doesn't turn away. He draws closer. He's the one who steps into the middle of your struggles and says, "I've got this. Let me help you."

Vulnerability can be scary, but it's also freeing. It's the moment you stop trying to hold everything together on your own and let God step in. It's the moment His peace fills the cracks and His power lifts the weight. You don't have to be perfect to experience His love—you just have to trust Him enough to let Him work through your imperfections.

So don't see your weaknesses as something to be ashamed of. They're not roadblocks; they're opportunities for God to show you just how strong He is. His grace is always enough. And His power? He perfects it precisely when you're at your weakest.

Practical Steps Toward Authentic Connection

You need to start with taking a closer look at where you might be holding back your vulnerability. Are there things you're afraid to share with a friend, a family member, or even God? If so, start small. Maybe it's telling someone you trust about something that's on your heart, joining a group where you feel safe being real, or just writing it out on paper. Taking these steps will help you to connect more deeply and honestly, not only with others but also with God.

Being vulnerable isn't about seeking pity or unloading every detail of your life. It's about creating space for real conversations that bring healing and understanding. When you share your struggles—like anxiety or doubt—with sincerity and faith, it shows others they're not alone. That kind of honesty speaks volumes about your strength, not weakness.

As you practice being open, invite God into those moments. When you surrender your struggles to Him, you're stepping into the trust that He will meet you right there. His grace brings healing and growth, even when it feels messy or uncomfortable. Vulnerability with God strengthens your spirit and shows you that you don't have to carry your burdens alone.

When you choose to be vulnerable, it creates a ripple effect. You will feel encouraged to share your own struggles, and the support that flows from those connections will feel like breathing fresh air. You celebrate victories together, lift each other up, and live God's love in action. Vulnerability doesn't make you weak; it makes you shine with God's grace. Being open builds stronger relationships, deepens your faith, and will help you find the strength that you didn't know you had.

Chapter 15: Healing Yourself by Helping Others

When you're stuck in your own anxiety, it's easy to forget the healing you get when you're helping others. There is incredible power in being able to help a friend through a struggle or to pray for someone who needs it. If you do, you may discover that your own heart is changed as well. It's almost as if you find a part of yourself that you thought was forgotten.

When you're there for someone going through a tough time, it's vitally important to take care of your own mental health, too. It's like filling someone else's cup with water, only to forget that your own cup is empty. Helping them out and being there for them is super important, but don't forget to look after yourself, too.

It's natural to think that we should always have the answers, right? We often want to be the one who fixes things, the person your loved one can come to for comfort and solutions. We want to make everything better for the people we love, and you do have the power to make a difference. It's important to acknowledge your emotional boundaries and take care of your energy levels. You can't be everything to everyone, no matter how much you want to help.

If you're not caring for yourself, it is tough to be fully present for others. Taking care of your own emotional, physical, and spiritual needs isn't selfish; it's wise. It's an act of love because when you stay strong and grounded, you're able to give more fully. It's easy to get swept up in their worry and stress. That's why it's so important to recognize when your emotional capacity is full and when to ask for extra support from a counselor or a mentor.

There are moments when the weight of someone else's struggles becomes too much for you to handle on your own. Don't be afraid to admit it and gently put in a boundary. In fact, it's better for everyone if you acknowledge when you need to stop helping others or know when to ask for it for yourself. Asking for support doesn't mean you've failed—it means you're smart enough to recognize that your strength comes from God, but He often works through others to support you, and that's not something to be ashamed of.

But how do you achieve that balance? It starts with awareness. So be honest with yourself about how you're feeling. Are you feeling drained? Overwhelmed? Sometimes you've been carrying someone else's burden for too long. It's okay to take a few steps back to breathe and recharge. It doesn't mean you don't care; it just means you're respecting your own limits. It's about finding ways to ensure you can stay there long-term without burning out.

If you're having trouble setting boundaries, don't be afraid to seek help. Here prayer can be an incredibly powerful tool. Ask God for wisdom on what to say, when to say it, when to listen, and when to step back. He knows that you want to help. He'll give you the strength to carry on.

Here's another difficult truth: You can't fix everyone's problems. As much as you'd like to, there are some things only they or God can do. Part of being a Christian is to support people in their struggles. Remember, though, the person you're helping must also be willing to do their own restorative work and ask God for healing.

So, when you are helping someone through their struggles, don't forget to check in with yourself. Are you okay? Are you exhausted, run down, or totally overwhelmed? If you are, it's time to step back and seek help. You can lean on God just like you encourage others to lean on God. Strength and calmness come from this balance of giving and receiving. It's not about doing it all; it's about giving what you have and letting God complete the rest.

Helping others is something you're no doubt called to do. Just remember that it doesn't necessarily mean sacrificing your well-being. Setting healthy boundaries and taking care of yourself means you'll be able to keep showing up to love others and to share the strength that God has given you. It doesn't mean you have to fix everything. It simply involves trusting God to handle the rest while you focus on what you can. If you are tired, don't wait to ask Him to fill your cup again. He's always willing to give you the strength to keep going.

Understanding the Importance of Boundaries

It's not easy finding the right balance between wanting to help and knowing your own limits. You might want to fix everything, to do all you can for the person you're supporting. But setting boundaries doesn't mean you're abandoning them—it just means you're figuring out what you can give without burning out. For instance, if you find that you are always reassuring someone, maybe politely suggest they get help (i.e., a counselor or a support group). It's possible to give the steady support they need without you having to do it all yourself.

You need to have open conversations about your boundaries. This doesn't need to be awkward or uncomfortable, but from experience, it isn't always something that people are willing to accept. This is especially so for narcissists. You have to frame it in a way that shows you still want to be there for them in a way that respects both of your needs. A simple and honest conversation like, "I'm happy to listen and talk with you, but I've found I'm most supportive when I have time each week to rest and pray. Let's figure out how we can make that work" sets a healthy expectation for everyone involved.

This is a favorable time to share your own self-care routines. It also shows that caring for themselves is just as important—so when you encourage them to do something similar, you're sending the right message. It's not about being perfect or having it all together all the time; it's just knowing we all need time to refresh. Both of you understanding and respecting each other's boundaries will keep your relationship strong and healthy.

Don't forget that Scripture can be a beautiful way to offer support. The Bible has many verses that tell you how important leaning on God's strength in the midst of struggle is. Sharing verses that talk of their unique challenges will keep your conversations in faith. The Bible is full of stories about people who had to trust God in difficult moments. Those stories can be a powerful reminder that it's okay to acknowledge your limits and trust God to be your strength.

By setting and respecting boundaries, you give both of you some space to feel cared for. You help them with compassion and balance for both of you. In setting boundaries, you actually get to be more present, more focused, and more intentional with your support. In the end, it makes you and the person you're walking alongside grow and heal in a sustainable and meaningful way.

Deeper Level Active Listening Techniques

Active listening is a beautiful way to bring peace to both yourself and others. When you choose to listen to (not merely hear) their words, you connect with their deepest feelings. It's not just being quiet when they talk; it's creating a space for them to feel safe to share what is truly happening in their heart.

At the heart of active listening is something called reflective listening. This means you show the person you've really understood them by restating or summarizing what they've said. For instance, if someone shares that they feel alone, you might say, "It sounds like you're feeling really isolated right now." That simple response shows them that you get it—that you're really hearing what they're feeling. It helps you break down their walls; you make an effort to understand them fully. By doing this, you'll often find them opening up even more.

There's more to active listening than your responses during a conversation. Subconscious messages can be communicated from little things like making eye contact or nodding. By looking someone in the eye, you show them your importance and give them your full attention. This can encourage them to continue talking to you. They also help build trust—they know it's a safe space to share without fear of being misunderstood.

Another way to help someone feel actually heard is by asking open-ended questions. Instead of asking yes or no questions, ask questions that get them thinking deeper. For example, 'What's been the hardest part for you?' "How are you feeling about everything right now?" They get a chance to really think about what's going on inside (sometimes realizing things they didn't even realize they were feeling). It's as if we're giving them space to work through their thoughts and gain clarity.

Sometimes silence is also as important as speaking. It's awkward, but it's nice to let someone sit in silence for a moment so that they can collect their thoughts or build up the courage to share something more profound. They might even spend some of those quiet moments working through feelings they hadn't fully processed yet. It's not forcing conversation, but it's about letting them have their time and space to speak at their own pace.

And here's something beautiful: Listening and providing support will be a part of your own healing. Spending time connecting with someone else's struggles can get you out of your own head. Their story can give you a new perspective on yours. It becomes a mutual exchange. You are helping them, and by being there for them, you are helping yourself.

Our calling as Christians is to love and support one another during difficult times. Living out that calling is as simple and powerful as active listening. When you combine faith with emotional and mental health practices, you can heal others and yourself.

Providing Scriptural Encouragement

Reading scripture has a way of healing that's deep and personal, both for you and for those you care about. The right Bible passages can help us through life's difficult moments. You have to find the words that will speak directly to someone's specific struggle and give them comfort that feels real and genuine.

For instance, if you know someone who's constantly overwhelmed, Matthew 11:28-30 can be especially comforting. Jesus says, *"Come to me, all you who are weary and burdened, and I will give you rest."* Guiding someone to verses like this can help them relate their challenges to something greater, something that endures.

Scripture becomes a tool for deep, personal healing when we really listen to what someone is going through. Instead of offering a verse that sounds like a one-size-fits-all solution, try to think about what that person needs right now. What are they feeling? What could they do to feel seen and understood? Listening and reflecting before sharing scripture builds trust, indicates compassion, and therefore makes God's word resonate more deeply.

It's a powerful step in the healing process to encourage someone to reflect on scripture. Maybe you could encourage them to journal or think about a verse that speaks to their situation. This isn't just about reading God's word; it's about God's message moving inside of them, becoming a part of their healing, not something they read from afar.

Everyone connects with scripture differently, and some do not connect at all. There's no one-size-fits-all interpretation. I never stop finding new layers of meaning in Bible verses. You know how we always picture Psalm 23 as a peaceful scene? I was just thinking about how it goes way deeper than that. That's when the whole *"walking through the valley of the shadow of death"* part becomes so real. David is assuring us that God is always there with us during our toughest times as well. It's amazing how a psalm can connect with us in such special ways depending on our experiences. Helping others see these different sides of scripture lets it come alive, meeting them exactly where they are.

As you walk alongside someone and share scripture with them, remember, your role isn't to have all the answers. You're there to help them make their own connection to God's word, to guide them toward finding how it speaks to their struggles. Gently guide them toward scripture and let them discover how God's word brings strength.

For many of us, it's challenging to balance everything life throws at us while holding onto our faith. With the Bible as your life companion, you'll gain wisdom and comfort. In every season, it is your trusted friend providing you exactly what your heart is longing for. It becomes a living, breathing truth that guides your emotional and spiritual healing.

The Message

As we wrap things up, remember this: Your help doesn't have to be perfect; it just has to be real. In this chapter, we talked about how to set appropriate boundaries and give gentle advice. The fact is, the only real support isn't about fixing everything; it's about being there in a way that is mindful of you and of them.

Two of the most powerful tools you have are active listening and sharing scripture that resonates with someone's heart. When you listen closely, you're giving someone the space to fully express themselves. And when you share scripture, you're giving them something that points them back to God.

You won't have all the answers, but being with someone may be all they need. What really matters is that you're there and showing that you care. Encouraging them to take time for themselves helps them to heal. Be kind and gentle, and God first.

There are opportunities to connect with each other in the conversations you have about faith and healing from anxiety. You're not just offering support; you're helping them connect with God in a way that speaks directly to where they're at. Vulnerability, trust, and compassion form a bridge between their faith and the healing they're looking for.

Ultimately, you're not trying to fix everything or make their pain go away. You're there to help them through their challenges. You don't need to have all the answers, but your presence and your empathy matter. By doing that, you give them the power to experience their own peace and healing.

*"Sometimes the most important
thing in a whole day
is the rest taken between
two deep breaths."*

~ Etty Hillesum ~

Chapter 16: Your Beautiful Future

As a Christian, dealing with anxiety, worry, fear, and depression can feel like a constant battle against invisible forces. However, in those difficult moments, beautiful things can happen—transition.

A balanced approach to managing anxiety brings together your faith, along with therapeutic tools and lifestyle changes. Imagine putting all the different parts of your life together—prayer, counseling, mindfulness, and having your community at your side. They all play a role in your healing.

Your relationship with God is the heart of it all. When you pray, you are inviting peace into your heart. You are allowing His presence to quiet your mind. Prayer is great, but pairing it with professional help when needed truly makes a world of difference. You aren't trying to replace your faith with psychology; you're adding tools to your spiritual toolbox. This opens your mind to face anxiety with more strength and courage.

Another big puzzle piece is community. It is essential to have people around you who get it, from your church, a support group, or even just a close friend who listens without judgment. It lightens your emotional load when you have others walking beside you. It's like coming out of the depths of isolation and into connection. You know you are not the only one struggling, and that knowledge can make such a difference.

There are so many practical ways to keep your anxiety in check. For instance, take a few deep breaths and pray when you get up in the morning. Things like practicing mindfulness during your day can keep you grounded. At night, spend a few minutes writing down the good things that happened that day. These small habits are a way to begin helping yourself get centered and find peace in the moment.

If you consistently practice these habits, they will make you more resilient. When your anxiety flares up, they become your go-to tools. Having a routine offers structure, and it's a way to strengthen both your mind and spirit. Imagine each day as a hill you must walk up. There are days when the incline will be steep and days when you feel like you're walking downhill instead. You're getting closer to peace with every step.

It's a slow process that you'll need to be patient with. Your small victories do add up. Trust that the process is going well, even if it seems to be slow. Every time you worry, you're taking yourself away from your faith. When you decide to release anxiety and believe in God's timing, you're making your spirit stronger.

I wish you the best as you use the tools in this book to help reduce your anxiety. It is possible to live a life free of anxiety, even if you don't feel that way right now. Be kind to yourself and know that God has you in His heart.

With love,
Grace.

Thank You for Reading!

I truly appreciate your support and the time you've taken to read this book! If you feel called to, please leave a review so other anxious Christians can find the help they need. Your words of love also help me as an author to inspire as many people as I can. Reviews don't have to be long—even a few sentences sharing your experience with the book make a big difference!

You can leave your review here: http://links.wingsofgracepublishing.com/anxiety-book or use the QR code below:

Turn Worry into Worship with this FREE guide

As a thank you for reading this book, I want to offer you the *'Hand Your Anxiety Over to God'* Surrender Plan. This simple guide will help you stop spiraling thoughts, find peace in His presence, and turn worry into worship.

I'd also love to gift you my 7-day mini-course on trusting and living in God's grace. It will automatically be delivered, along with the guide.

Download the guide here:

https://wingsofgracepublishing.com/surrender/

or use the QR code below:

What's Next?

Consider surrendering your anxious thoughts as part of a daily devotion.

The companion daily devotional to this book *From Worry to Worship: A 52-Week Devotional Bible Study for Anxiety* will help you.

Sometimes it may feel very hard, but each time you surrender, you move that much closer to peace.

You can find it on Amazon or through my website here: https://wingsofgracepublishing.com/from-worry-to-worship-devotional-for-anxiety/

About the Author

Grace Andrews is a Christian author passionate about sharing the transformative power of faith through inspirational writing. With a heart for spiritual growth, she offers readers practical insights and biblical wisdom to help them navigate life's challenges.

She is fueled by coffee and the love of her husband of 25 years. She adores international travel, quiet moments with God, reading, and creating. Grace both writes and designs all of her own books, including the covers and interior layout.

Grace believes that God's love and guidance can lead anyone to greater peace, purpose, and fulfillment.

Find out more about Grace and her books here:

https://wingsofgracepublishing.com/

Reference List

Ede, D.G. (2019). The Carnivore Diet for Mental Health? [online] Psychology Today. Available at: https://www.psychologytoday.com/blog/diagnosis-diet/201904/the-carnivore-diet-for-mental-health [Accessed 13 Jan. 2025].

Kiltz, R. (2023). Carnivore Diet Probiotics: The Facts. [online] Doctor Kiltz. Available at: https://www.doctorkiltz.com/carnivore-diet-probiotics/.

Norton, S. (2023). Little known facts about oxalates and their poisonous effects. [online] Sally K. Norton. Available at: https://sallyknorton.com/oxalate-science/.

Shetty, M. (2024). More Than a Gut Feeling: How Your Microbiome Affects Your Mood | Gut Health. [online] Lifestyle Medicine. Available at: https://longevity.stanford.edu/lifestyle/2024/04/08/more-than-a-gut-feeling-how-your-microbiome-affects-your-mood/.

www.ingramcontent.com/pod-product-compliance
Lightning Source LLC
Chambersburg PA
CBHW072018070526
44583CB00015B/1529